YOU ARE THE CHOICES YOU MAKE

BRIAN ABBEY

PAGE PUBLISHING, INC.
New York, NY

First originally published by Page Publishing, Inc. 2015

ISBN 978-1-68213-544-0 (pbk)
ISBN 978-1-68213-545-7 (digital)

Printed in the United States of America

INTRODUCTION

You Are the Choices You Make!

When I was originally inspired to write this book seven years ago, I was thirty-seven years old. To date I was adept at overcoming adversity. From living on my own at fifteen, drop out at sixteen, arrested three times by seventeen, and father at eighteen. Nineteen years later I was full of my meager accomplishments of building a construction company working for established clients doing twenty million in revenues, acquiring and developing a real estate company with my wife, and getting our first child off to the college of her choice.

Did I have an inspiring story to tell? Yes. But instinctively I knew the story was not ready to be told. My drive to write and or inspire was not going to come from my meager accomplishments. At that time all I could do was tell of the success. Anyone can go to Amazon and purchase a number of books on the subject of success. Reading the inspirational insights of authors on success, there are many that I enjoyed like Og Mandino, Napoleon Hill, Robert Kiyosaki, to name a few. That is not the story I wanted to tell. The story that burned inside me was that of social awareness based on my experiences with a plethora of different but similar people that cross race, religion, and financial status lines.

Beyond telling my story, which is certainly not worthy of an autobiography, I always felt I had a unique insight to share. Like most reading this book, we have the ability to study and reflect on the nature of people we encounter. Growing up in the Bronx, New York, there is no shortage of people to study. In fact in my short forty-four years to date, I can honestly say that I have encountered the best and the worst of human conditions in that environment. Moreover, the social conditions that you encounter growing up in an urban environment have inspired the social message of this book. As we will experience together, overcoming adversity does not make you unique. Overcoming being average does!

You might ask yourself, if we are all sharing the same experiences in life, then why don't we arrive at the same destination or achieve the same measure of success. Some would argue that we all react differently to situations. That line of thinking is for those that have no control over their lives! Ask yourself why children raised by the same parents wind up in different directions in life. How do some people rise above their social standings when they are growing up in substandard means like hundreds of thousands of people their age?

Should you take the time to finish this book, you will be able to answer these questions. In this book we will analyze the only consistent factor in success and failure. Choice. Choice is the opportunity to reflect how we really see ourselves. Choice is the opportunity to put our principles into action. Sadly many people are not even aware that they are making a choice. Society has tricked us that we are just giving in to impulses. You're not. Your choice may be ill advised, your choice may be contrary to how you were raised or what you believe, but it still your choice. After you have finished this book, you may never look at the personal decision making process the same way again.

My hope for this book is that of social awareness. Recent generations have taken the focus away from accountability and placed the focus on finding someone to blame. This book will demand personal accountability. On reading this book my desire is that we will (you and I) awaken a deeper reflection into the social condition. We will reflect on our choices. We will come to the conclusion that all we have and all we will become is a matter of the choices we make.

Your life changes when your choices do. Commit your character to accountability and make choices moving forward that reflect that character.

We will also discover that using your values and character does not always manifest into the desired success initially. As you will read, my character and subsequent choices had some disastrous consequences. I do believe in an often-posted quote, "Life is 10 percent of what happens to us and 90 percent of how we react to it." Through reflecting on success and failures of my own, I was forced to ask why. The answers to that insight have inspired this book.

Please be aware that an academic or a professional author is not writing this book. Before writing an outline I wanted to come up with an adjective to guide the style in which I would write. The word that came to mind was relatable. My desire was that any reader from eighteen to sixty can see their life in some way in these pages. In an effort to be relatable, I felt that I should keep the chapters brief. You will note that I am using a more educated syntax to get my point across in the first person point of view. Do not be fooled by the written word. I am from the street. The stories and the wisdom are borne from the street. Anyone that knows me personally can see that it was a struggle to stay brief. As you will read each chapter can stand on its own.

For the first three chapters we review the process and the tools of analyzing choice. From 4 through 6 we will review a few different types of choices. From chapters 7 through 12 we will review factors from unforeseen circumstances to the conversation in our mind that affect our choices. The book *will not* tell you what the correct choice is. A correct choice for one person is not the same for another. This book will allow you the perspective and the tools to make the best choice for you. In the event that you are looking for another product to validate you as a victim, this book is not for you. This book is a vehicle to give you the best opportunity to do what is right for you.

Lastly, the book is neither an autobiography nor a self-help book. The book is about observations and piecing together the social condition we live in. Think of this book as an opportunity to see yourself in every page. Upon reading you will relive the factors and choices that led to your best decisions as well as your worst.

One of the goals of this book is to allow you to see that you are the choices you make. Despite what the media and government will have you believe, you are only a victim of your own choices. There is no one to blame! You are the choices you make! Period! So now we are ready to discover through these pages we are all the authors of our own life. When we finish this book, we will have the perspective to write new chapters.

CHAPTER ONE

Choice. Principles in Action

Choice is described in *Webster's Dictionary* as an (noun) "opportunity or privilege to choose freely." Let those words sink in for a moment. Then now notice that this word is a noun. Given this word is not a person, place, or thing, then it must be an idea. Idea is also a noun that the same dictionary describes as a "plan of action or intention." So basically our ideas and subsequent choices about situations and matters are the basic component of our existence. Imagine your life as a particle. Then the basic and beginning of your life is the atom, or as this chapter describes it, choice.

Since the time we could walk, our parents would coach us on making good decisions: "Stay away from the hot stove," "Look both ways before you cross the street." We became programmed in such a way that we were doing as we are told, albeit keeping us from danger. As we grow and mature we are taught principles guided by morals. We were taught to tell the truth, respect others and their property, and with hard work all goals can be achieved. Something happens about this time in your journey in life. You hit adolescence and your friends become more of a guide than your parents. In some cases this is not always bad. The real trouble with this route is your friends are feeling their way through life just like you. As different as we are, amazingly we all go through the same phases in life.

Now in the life of social media and sensationalism, our perspective as to what is real and pertinent has gone by the wayside. We do without thinking, as we believe in effect that this helps us to blend in. Today's YOLO (*you only live once*) generation has completely abandoned "thinking things through" part in life as the parents today make all responsible decisions in spite of a child doing what they want in lieu of what they need. Worse yet, there are no consequences. Basically there is no scorecard for your choice. We will delve into this subject in subsequent chapters.

As I mentioned in the introduction, most people are not even aware that they are making a choice. We just slowly build up what I call default behavior. Sadly, most people's default behavior is subterfuge. The act of blaming people and bringing up a myriad of issues that are not related to the bad choice the complainant made. So there is no scorecard, no correction, just a blend of poor decisions that the person living them is not aware; regardless of who's to blame, he or she will live the consequences. *The first part of making a good choice is to know you are making one.*

I am asking you now to be aware of every choice you make for the next three days. No matter how mundane the decision before you, promise you will at least recognize *you* are making a choice. Become acquainted with that little voice inside your head. That is your conscience and it is very wise. In every chapter of this book we will touch on one consistent reality. The reality is *you* are the choices you make. Should you choose to save a percentage of your income, you are guaranteed to have a savings account (a choice that I highly recommend). Should you choose to finance your way through life, then you will be in debt and labeled financially irresponsible. When you get in your car after having five beers and two scotches and get pulled over, whose fault is it? Are you really a victim of an overzealous police officer? *No.* Again, you are the choices you make. The good news is starting tomorrow we can make different choices. Ones we know we will be held accountable for, therefore taking time to consider the pros and cons.

As I mentioned earlier, our parents have been teaching us basic principles to live a successful life. I am not saying that our parents lived their own advice. Having said that every parent wants their children to be more and better than themselves, and they act and guide accordingly. Our parents were our first mentors. Again parents taught us honesty, work ethic, treating others how you want to be treated. While this book is not here to reteach all the proper principles, it is written to get you to start considering them. While I for one will never excuse children making the same mistakes as their parents, I do understand them. For most of my life I have smoked cigarettes. I know it is wrong. I am fully aware of the consequences. Worst yet, I am not happy ever having been addicted to nicotine.

We mentioned earlier about default behavior. This is the behavior that we result to without thinking of the consequences. We do this for several reasons. For one, we might have had success or experienced a desired result by lying. We might have grown up with a parent who abused alcohol. In many cases, we observed the habits of our parents and family and repeated all manners of behavior because it seemed to fit the norm. So in many cases our parents' behavior can shape a level of acceptable behavior that may not be appropriate in the world you now live in. Worst yet, most people are not even aware that they are repeating the patterns.

Moving forward it may be wise to look back and analyze the factors of our choices and if we were really aware that we were making them or acting in a manner that was accepted in a particular circle.

In retrospect, look at your own teenage years to analyze the choices you made and their effects. Good place to start since most reading this book will have had at least experienced these years. Would your life be different if you made different choices? Were you aware at the time of making the choice that the consequences would have been so prominent in your future? I would like to share a few of my critical decisions that I made at this juncture of my life that absolutely shaped my future.

At the time that I spent three years in high school, I had worked, saved, and enjoyed nights out with friends. Speaking of friends, we have an amazing ability to analyze their decisions. We need to use that same ability on ourselves. When I was a teenager, I partied with friends and experimented with drugs. Definitely not my best decision. There was a slight difference. I was willing to take the risk in a controlled environment like my apartment. There is a street principle that mandates, "Do not shit where you eat." Basically the premise is you can take risk, just not in your neighborhood. Do not dishonor yourself where your family lives. Fortunately I respected myself, and my friends respected me when I refused to engage in activity that involved parties and vehicles. By no means was I a nerd or nervous. I grew up in an environment where it was important that you had your wits about you at all times. I respected the principles of the street and made a choice not to violate the rules. I chose never to be in public with a weakened state of reason. This decision served me well. I cannot say the same for all my friends.

By the age of eighteen, I had already been living on my own for three years. I dropped out of high school for reasons a rational adult could never print. I knew it was the wrong decision. In lieu of an education I resolved something that day. No one would out work me…ever. Anyone that came in contact with me would remember how hard I worked. Perhaps I could earn enough in time to go back to college as I loved academia. This never materialized, as I would be a father a month before my nineteenth birthday. Once again a result from a bad decision (not wearing a condom). You are the choices you make, and now I was a father. I never looked at my unusual situation and felt bad for myself (a choice society today would understand me making). Instead I was invigorated by the new possibility and opportunity to establish the ultimate accomplishment, raising a child. So if there is ever a time to be aware of your choices and consequences long term, it is when you are faced with being a parent. My life could have taken many different directions if I was not aware that my choices affected many lives, not just my own. So I left a $60,000 union job in New York in 1990 to be a $35,000 a year superintendent in Florida. You are the choices you make. I wanted to be away from the influences and loyalties that the Bronx provided. We left our family and friends and left no retreat. This was a choice I knew would be benefit my new family.

While making $60,000 was a good living for a twenty-year-old in New York, I was motivated by my principles of giving my family the best environment, not the easiest one for me. Money was never part of my decision. Principles were. Once again your choices must become your principles in action no matter the sacrifice. I made a choice to follow my vocation into construction. Yes it was my decision! Crazy, huh? For those reading this not in the construction field, it is fair to say that a full 70 percent of us had no intention of doing this type of work when we left high school or college. We took a summer job. We made four times the minimum wage was and said, "Why should I follow my dreams, I am making good money here. I will do it later." So while Danielle and I lived week to week, I took jobs to learn, not to earn. My choice was the construction field. My choice was not to be average. Principles I acted on. So I spent the next four years learning all I could to further my ambitions to learn all the trades. I chose to read books on every trade, not watch TV. I chose different positions of purchaser, superintendent, estimator, and project manager. All the while we were falling further in debt as my salaries did not exceed my expenses. After spending my four years in the college of life I only had $18,000 of debt. Not even owning a car I could have gone bankrupt, but that choice would have helped a short-term issue and created years of regret. I chose to work my way out of debt on weekends and nights. None of these choices were easy. What made them satisfying is that they were conscience choices, choices made after contemplation.

So after four years we are $18,000 in debt and we now needed a home as we had our son thirty months later in 1991. Ashley would start school in a year, so more choices were to be made. Danielle and I set out to eradicate our debt. We wanted to be homeowners. So that meant having the requisite funds homeowners had, good credit, and living below our means to get there. Seems easy, some may agree. These are tough choices. We did not drive a new car via the finance company. We did not eat out anywhere ever! Basically beyond food we did not buy anything that did not make us money. Eighteen short months later we had no debt but for the $90,000 mortgage on our home. You are the choices you make. This was not one choice but three choices a day that helped shape this reality. Every day we made choices not to compromise our future for things we thought we needed now.

For those of us with small children reading this book, here is a small insight we all take for granted. Make your children aware that they are making choices and there are consequences. Your children are the choices they make. They are also the friends they keep. Make them aware. If they are older than fourteen, make them read the book. Remind them A students would be B students if they choose to play video games instead of study. The road to confidence to reach our goals is not a long one if you are willing to commit your character to the right principles and make choices to put those principles in action. Make a go of it tomorrow. Set a goal for the week and make every choice to benefit that goal. Dare yourself not to be average. You have gifts to offer the world. What is your goal? Set it and make all the series of small choices that add up to the sum of your dream. Just make sure it is made with the right principles that put your choice into action.

CHAPTER 2

Cause and Effect

After saving 20 percent of his income for twelve years Charles bought his home with cash. Charles was able to save because he had no credit cards or financed automobiles. Upon buying the house, Charles discovered that repairs were needed to the roof. Having no credit history, no money could be advanced, and in four short months the hole was made larger and his new home was flooded.

We all studied these examples of cause and effect since elementary school. Sadly we lost the analytical skill somewhere along the way. Let's review. Charles buying a new home (effect) was a result of him saving 20 percent of his income (cause). As universal law dictates a seed of good holds its equivalent; opposite, bad. Since he was so careful at not wasting money on interest, when he needed money, it was not available. Repairs were needed to a roof that flooded the house (effect). No established credit hindered his ability to borrow funds (cause).

I apologize to the readers because the examples seem, well, elementary. The common sense of the issues at hand screams, "Of course…that makes sense." Glad you agree because in this chapter we are going to hammer home how little we use a skill taught from grade school to college. In the last chapter we discussed identifying what choices we made and to recognize how many choices we make in one day. In this chapter I want to tap into a skill that we can utilize daily in reflecting on our choices that can aid us in the future to make better ones.

Like any other skill, this too takes practice. In an effort to practice we need situations. Well, this will be easy, as a normal life of our own, as well as friends and family, gives us no shortage of situations. Then we will need tools to work on analyzing these situations. The tools I recommend are common sense as in the issue depicted above. We will also need to use emotionless rationale. However, none of our tools will work unless we have the vision to do our work. So we will need light! In this case of using our work metaphor the light that is needed to illuminate the situation to use rationale and common sense is honesty!

Of all the friends and enemies you will encounter in your life, no one will deceive you more than you! Why? The reason is we easily mislead our thoughts to shade our involvement in our bad choices. You know this is true. That is why we don't acknowledge we are making choices. We do not look at the cause and effect that forced us to choose or analyze the consequences of the choice. Instead we blame the effect for all. In keeping with our example, let's use Charlie again. Let's assume that because Charlie acted so responsibly saving his money that he believes he knows everything. So when something bad happened, Charlie blamed the prior owners for not disclosing the leak, blamed the bank for not recognizing his financial accomplishment, blamed the roofer who wanted too much money. Had Charlie used common sense, rationale, and honesty, his thoughts would have led him to a quicker conclusion. Lesson for us all, taking time for pity and blame is time wasted correcting the issue. Thus, had he been honest, he would have said I should have paid another five hundred for a home inspection and now I need to research multiple ways to get funding to deal with my issue in an expeditious manner. So as we reflect on Charlie's issue, we can deduce the following: Charlie is a hardworking, responsible guy. Like all people in life with a new experience, he made mistakes. A mistake that was made far worse due to his inability to be honest with himself and take immediate corrective action. Is this starting to sound familiar? Good, because if you're going to continue, you really need to be honest, brutally honest. So let's end this paragraph with one more bit of common sense. You cannot analyze or correct an issue unless you admit your part in it. That's called learning.

In honestly using cause-and-effect analysis we can build an environment around us that puts us in a position to succeed. Through accepting our responsibility and role in situations as the cause, we can learn not to put ourselves in a position to fail. Thereby avoiding the negative effect. Conveniently growing up in the environment of the Bronx, this becomes instinctive to the successful ones. A quick example would be going to bars and clubs with friends. On the surface this seems like a benign activity. Unfortunately, when there is liquor, immaturity, and loyalty, you find your principles compromised one too many times. So after getting arrested a few times for assault you stop focusing on the effect (fight) and look at the cause. The cause was running with a crowd that was always out to have a good time. We never wanted issues, but with the liquor, immaturity, and the testosterone and estrogen environment of a club or bar, trouble is inevitable. Again while we were never an instigator, I was more than willing to finish. So I decided not to put myself in positions to fail and stopped being in that environment with close friends. While this situation will not fit all people in their teenage years, we can all think of like kind scenarios.

The bottom line is we are all very different people with default behaviors that are part of our matrix. The above example illustrates that I am not one to hide from confrontation. Thus, I learned not to put myself in a position where my negative default behavior would manifest. Instinctively we all can avoid being in a situation or place where we do not want to be. The real trick is to avoid where we want to be, because our personality or default behavior enhances the ability to make bad decisions. For the parents or younger generation reading this book, take it as a sign of maturity that you accept your faults and live your life not to put yourself in environments that they will manifest. A more direct comparison would be an alcoholic. They may be good employees, husbands, wives, and friends; however, if they put themselves in the wrong environment, they fail! This example is common sense. Now apply that same common sense to your own shortcomings (we all have a few). Should this analysis aid in your future choices?

Believe that using cause-and-effect analysis will always aid you in the ability to make sense of your past as well as your future. This does not mean you will make the right choices. What it will do is accept your role in any given situation. Deep down you know who you are. You can change the way you look at your life. Through this analysis you can change your circumstances and maybe how you accept the role your choices play in your life.

While we are on the subject of change and cause and effect, I would like to state the obvious. You cannot change other people. Period. You journey is yours, not theirs. People will not change who they are to adapt to you. As I have mentioned several times in this book thus far, our YOLO, self-absorbed generation will do well to embrace this notion. Unfortunately, this generation is too self-absorbed and hypocritical when it comes to this issue. All generations have self-absorbed, rebellious teenagers. The only difference is this generation somehow believes that grown adults, parents, and teachers and employers should adapt to their needs. Worse, they are incensed with a sense of entitlement when anyone does not acquiesce to their needs or feelings. Only through being honest with your own faults can you have empathy for others.

I will give an example of being a parent of a teenager that all can relate to that ties in to this chapter as well as the generation that we have mentioned. In this example, I will use my daughter who was twenty-two at the time. The disclaimer to the story is to know that while true it is in no way indicative of my relationship with my daughter. Our relationship is beyond special. Having said that, I will speak on it as we can all relate to both sides and use our cause-and-effect analysis with common sense, rationale, and honesty.

My daughter was visiting my wife and me with three friends from college. Weeks to arriving she had asked if I can arrange a room at the local casino so she could go to the club with friends. Naturally I obliged. Knowing I would be there to check her in, I too made plans with friends to meet for dinner in a local restaurant. Now before I explain the rest of the story, know that I am a huge stickler for time, punctuality, and respect. Also terribly predictable, meaning my reaction can absolutely be anticipated. Being of Italian descent it is drilled in you to respect family wishes, especially when they are doing something for you. To continue, my daughter arrived twenty minutes late, thereby making me late. Of course I called my guest to inform them. My daughter, on the other hand, did not. All I knew was that they were shopping. We were to meet at 8:00 p.m. in the lobby. I would get there early to check in and get room keys for her and three friends. Being a cool dad I also arranged free passes to that club that evening. When my daughter arrived twenty minutes late, I was furious at the utter disrespect for me as well as the kindness I had shown my daughter and her friends. So I did what any disrespected Italian father would do. I let her know about it. *No* I did not scream in the lobby, but if you were within five yards, you could hear me as well as have your eyebrows singed from the heat coming off my head. My daughter was furious with embarrassment and at me for her perceived slight. She took her keys and did not talk to me for two weeks in spite of staying at our house for the next four days.

So let's use our cause-and-effect analysis to see both sides. The effect was being angry at her lack of respect (maybe different to you, we raise our kids our way). The cause, her being late and not caring enough about other people's feelings to call; the effect for me was she did not talk to me and I missed quality time with her. The cause was letting my emotions get the better of me and not picking another time and place to address the situation. Both people had valid points. Except for a few simple points that elude YOLOs. One, I am truly consistent in my ways and manner. My daughter having been raised by me as well as having made jokes about my need for punctuality knew exactly what to expect. Unfortunately she was with three other YOLOs who acted in kind, and she felt that I would not call her out in front of her peers. She made a series of bad choices that day. She could have explained the time frame to her friends. She could have explained her dad to her friends, or she simply could have called to express regret and make alternate plans. No good decisions were made. I can say that in retrospect, if made to do it all over again, she would choose differently and so would I. The point of the story is you have to look at cause and effect. Teen readers, I am willing to bet if your parents overreact, it is due to the five times before that you did the same thing. Only this time you want to overreact as your parents did, so this somehow makes you right. Cause, you did not listen the first five times; effect, your parents reacted, and the criminal judges the victim. Out of balance. Parents be parents. Try explaining cause and effect to your children. Young ones know. No parent wants to be mean to their child. Use cause and effect to assess your roll. Then make different choices.

While writing this book our country endured the tragic deaths of Mike Brown in Ferguson, Missouri, and Freddie Gray in Baltimore, Maryland, at the hands of local police. Again just typing it and reading it is chilling indeed. Emotional to say the least. My issue is we get stunned with the emotion of this type of news and we immediately react to the effect (dead citizen) and ignore the cause. Our hearts and mind have already been played with before the logic part of our brain says "There must be a reason for this!" Police handling close to thirty millions stops and twelve million arrests every year do not look to kill the people they are protecting. The stats tell this crystal clear story. So after the media is done showing you a picture of Mike Brown, the fourteen-year-old innocent boy, and the loving uncle Freddy, we are forced to acknowledge cause. In both cases, both men's actions put themselves in a position to endure a fate never considered.

To be clear neither man deserved to die. This chapter is not on equality. The chapter is on cause and effect. Mike Brown being nineteen years old 6' 3" 270lbs, beating up a store clerk on video while being stoned is not a good decision and certainly cause for a plethora of negative effects to his life. Now the same Mike Brown (see size above) rejects a confrontation with the officer investigating a robbery. Another bad choice and cause for police to further investigate. Then punching the same police officer repeatedly to the face while he sits parked in a police vehicle. I would submit that the cause was Mike Brown's decisions and actions led to the effect, the police used deadly force out of fear. The author is the judge. The author is merely using a well-known incident as a measure of how to apply cause and effect to your life decisions as well as others.

Moving forward I would submit that the cause is every bit as important as the effect. We must correct our mistake and always consider the cause instead of focusing on the victimization of the effect. Through the analysis of the above examples we always find a seed of accountability in all things that touch our lives. All we need to do now is be honest.

CHAPTER 3

Accountability

What does it really mean to be accountable?? We know that we have to answer to our teachers, parents, and employers. In the event we answer with sincerity, I guess that is a measure of being accountable. We know that when we give someone our word, we must keep it. There is a measure of accountability to that. How about personal accountability? Do you hold yourself accountable and to what measure? Do you feel a sense of responsibility for what happens in your life? If the answers to this question are yes, then I will assume that you have a high degree of integrity. When speaking in terms of holding yourself accountable, then that is integrity. There is a quote on integrity that is spot on and it goes, "Integrity is doing the right thing when no one is looking." Basically it is a moral code and compass that we are given but somehow conveniently lose.

So for the purpose of this chapter, let's use the words *accountability* and *integrity* as the same word. We all have morals, albeit some people are lacking, or differ, but we all have morals. Whether you have children or will be a parent someday, morals come into play. There is a moral code we would teach our children about what is expected of gentlemen, or a lady. There is a moral code in dealing with finances and agreements that would be taught. While I can fill this chapter on morals and principles, I will not. You are on the third chapter of this book, so you know where I am going. The question is, what do you do when it all goes wrong? What do you do when the consequences compromise your morals? This is where accountability to yourself comes in. What you do with your back against the wall! The decision or choices you make when you can win by compromising your integrity or be accountable to yourself and your values.

On a personal note, I know a lot about accountability. As an emancipated youth at fifteen, things did not always go smooth. As an eighteen-year-old boy who played a huge part in impregnating his fifteen-year-old girlfriend, not a good time. As a twenty-five-year-old project manager building hotels, things did not always go smooth. When my wife and I built a twenty-million-dollar-a-year business with no money, things were never smooth. In fact when I opened the construction company, I never sold sticks and bricks. I sold accountability! Anyone can build. Hundreds of billions are spent on construction worldwide without me. I just wanted to keep my word to my clients and I did for thirteen straight years. As we will read later in this chapter, accountability in any form is expensive. Having said that, I never ran from my responsibilities...ever. Do you want to know why? The reason is simple. I made choices. Some bad ones, but they were mine. So after analyzing cause (choice) and effect (consequences), I was honest with myself and stuck to my moral code to assist in new choices. Accountability.

I believe that it is most important to note that all the things we speak of have no monetary value. Spirituality and a moral code do not have dollar values attached to them. The accountability we speak of is treating others how you want to be treated no matter how big the sacrifice. This is going to be essential if you are going to hold yourself accountable. Where I came from, that is all that mattered. Accountability has no monetary value in a physical manner of speaking. The intrinsic values are endless. One such value is respect. More directly I speak about the respect for you. Through holding yourself accountable for your choices, you will attain a greater respect for yourself and your ability to be someone worthy of respect. Another such value is reliability. Now this value through accountability does make you money. Whether you're an employee or an owner. Clients and employers want reliable people to work with. These types of people are always rewarded with more opportunities to earn. So holding yourself accountable for your choices does have a monetary value in life. Let's remember, the sword always cuts both ways. You just have to be comfortable with the choices you make either way.

Growing up in the Bronx no one was wealthy. Some had enough money to have no worries, but no one was wealthy. The currency in my neighborhood was respect. Respect for your ability to represent your family and neighborhood. Respect for your academic or sports prowess. Respect for being able to handle yourself in the street. The highest respect was for those that kept their word. Without knowing or understanding accountability or integrity this value permeated everything we did as a child. Some could say the need and demand for respect was suffocating in this environment. Maybe, but it resonated in me. I thrived in that environment. Thus, I feel grateful to grow up where and when I did to tap into this essential important skill.

In keeping with our introduction, let's be aware of the social awareness and benefits of being accountable. "Birds of a feather flock together." When you hold yourself accountable, you have no time for people that make excuses. When you hold yourself accountable through thoughts and deed, you will see your life and ability to love in a different manner that you do today. Your ability to empathize with people will be more acute. The reason for this is you will not be part of a group. You will see yourself as an individual who is an asset to the group. We need to attain this skill moving forward. We need to stop being hypocrites when it comes to situations in our life. Allow me to give you a simple metaphor for the consistency of integrity. All of us have electricity in our homes. We all expect that the electric will do as we ask by a simple touch of a finger. We expect it! Period. Guess what? They expect to be paid at the end of the month. Period! The fact that "they don't need your money" has nothing to do with the agreement and service you take for granted. You may have made some bad choices; you may have gotten caught up in other people's bad choices. This does not matter. You agreed to pay the bill. Pay it.

Don't complain. Don't cheat. Get another job…but pay it. While this example is very broad, you can apply it to all things in life.

While we are speaking of life and accountability I want to share some insights into the world we live in. I believe if we all acted in a manner of being accountable for our own lives, this alone can cure many social issues. Assuming you're intelligent enough to read this book, you are intelligent enough to understand the next few paragraphs.

All of us are shaped by our experiences. We choose in what manner. My mother took on the responsibility of being a single parent when I was two. She raised my brother and me with no formal education in a four-hundred-square-feet basement apartment on government subsidy, a.k.a. welfare/food stamps. Being a woman of character and wanting to set a good example for her children she used the assistance from government programs to get a GED and associates degree at Mercer College. This enabled her to get gainful employment for a living wage for her family. This accomplishment was dampened by the state threatening to take her children, as she would be an unfit mother, not being home for her kids. In the end she persevered. My mother went on to work till I was twenty-two. I consider myself lucky to be raised by a woman who had integrity in abundance. To say we never had extras would be to diminish the fact that we never had enough to pay bills. She believed in paying her bills. Moreover, she would not even present an expired coupon in the supermarket. That's integrity!

Sadly today's society and government has been way too slack on accountability. So without using this social measure, in my opinion we have a society that has run amok. Before I write down my rant on the social ills, know I am neither a democrat nor a republican as I am socially liberal and fiscally conservative. My observation on the lack of accountability will start with welfare and end with all of us. The reason for starting here is because I lived it. Presently we have a government that believes it is aiding its citizens by ingratiating people with welfare. After the money is allocated, there are no accountable measures to ensure that this assistance is being used as a proactive manner to integrate the people back into a productive lifestyle. Thus, the recipients are not accountable for their means and their lives. We know this to be true because we presently have three generations in a family on government assistance. To me the government is to empower, not ingratiate. So people who receive with no accountability feel there is no need to hold themselves accountable as they have a convenient scapegoat for all their ills, the government. The same way a child blames a parent for things they do not have. Worse we now have schools that do not hold themselves accountable. The parents blame teachers; teachers build parents. Tragically we have everyone blaming each other and we are so busy blaming one another that no one is watching what the government is doing to our constitution or the people's rights they pledged to protect.

People have the right to know they can support their family. People have the right to know they are equal to a person who works for what they have. Imagine if for three years we hold ourselves accountable for our circumstances. Imagine we as a country go for three years without blaming someone. Imagine if we take ownership of our choices and realize nothing would change till our choices do. Everyone needs help, rich or poor, black or white, Christian or Jew. In the paragraph above, I used the parent/child analogy. I want to *help* my children. I will *not* do for them. So when I do help them, I always ensure a measure of accountability. My children don't call it help. They call it a deal.

Let's look at circumstance, choice, and accountability in a more personal experience. What are the chances of someone succeeding after enduring the following bullet points?

- Raised in a single parent home
- Lived on welfare and food stamps as a child
- No high school education
- Arrested three times by age seventeen
- Child out of wedlock at eighteen

By our government's measure any two of the five would doom anyone to failure. You have probably already guessed all five of those bullet points were my life. Only difference was I was aware that I had choices. Not that I received the motivation from my political leaders. No, just a simple measure of holding myself accountable for my actions. When my girlfriend (later my wife) gave birth to our daughter, she was a fifteen-year-old girl with no education and no husband. We could have chosen not to marry for government convenience. Danielle would have been given rent money, welfare assistance, food stamps, free baby food—the works. Instead we chose a life of production. We chose a life of relying on our own efforts and pledged to live with the consequences. Help would have been nice, but we already know it's not help. It is an abandonment of the human spirit if not kept in check. So in summation the circumstances in two of the bullet points set the wheels in motion for the next three. The only thing that saved me was knowing better choices could bring better results. In spite of the hardship and all the easy ways that could be taken, I stayed and lived my choice. In short I was accountable for my actions. The reward, I won the respect of my best friend and partner, my wife Danielle. Sometimes in our search for treasure we do not see the jewel right under our nose.

One more benefit lost on society and enjoyed by those who wish to be accountable. Your mind! You become much sharper when you know that it is up to you to ensure the desired results of your choices. When you hold yourself accountable and blame no one for nothing, your mind moves past *survive* and you start to think about *thrive*! Holding yourself accountable means that your respect for you grows. Your children may learn from watching you what it means to be productive. Your spouse or family may be inspired by your willingness to be counted on. Even more you are happy they expect it because you sure as hell do. Know you're making choices, make them, live them, analyze them, and blame no one. Only then will you be living the life the Creator intended.

CHAPTER 4

"I Cannot Decide"

The truth is I really had no title for this chapter. Just kidding. The real truth is the statement when it comes to life's choices is paralyzing. All of us have experienced the state of being unable to make a choice. The older we get, the harder the choices get. What happens as we get smarter and more mature? Shouldn't the choices become easier? Of course we know the answer is no. When we are adolescents, the choices, experiences, and consequences are not as severe. Thus, most people are not risk adverse. As soon as we hit twenty-one-year-old legal adulthood we understand we are liable for consequences and can no longer use age as an excuse. At this time we become more aware of other people's choices than our own. So we begin to live with not only our own experiences but also the experiences of friends and family.

In the previous chapters we learned to be aware that we are making choices. We learned how to analyze our choices and how to live with them. Before we pat ourselves on the back that we can now make better choices, let's look at the worst choice of all. No choice. Indecision. So let's tie in the first three chapters. We do acknowledge our choices (cause) and role in consequences. Then we must acknowledge that the possible effect is scary. Thus, we must also acknowledge our part in the cause. Choice. Prior to reading this book, when things would go wrong, you would blame the effect and others. Now we are forced to acknowledge through our decisions that we play a huge part in the outcome of our own lives.

Is no decision better than making a wrong one? Well, academically, that depends on the consequences. Sadly my experience with indecision is usually borne of weakness and doubt. When making fear-based decisions, I would say more study is needed. That does not mean we procrastinate. How do we get rid of fear? How do you convince yourself that you are making the right choices that you can live with? For the rest of this chapter we will study factors that lead to indecision and the tactics that are essential to defeat this counterproductive condition. What is it about fear that makes it paralyzing?

By the time I was sixteen I had been hit with a baseball bat three times. Do I fear being hit with a baseball bat? No. I have lived the experience. I know the worst of it. Am I afraid to get hit with a bat? Yes. For instance, we all know someone who is afraid of hard work. Basically they had an experience where they felt the work was exhausting, and they wish not to repeat the experience. Therefore they are "afraid." When you have no experience with the perceived outcome, there is fear. In a street sense, all fear is, is not knowing. Know this in no way diminishes the emotional effects of fear. Try to visualize this effect. Remember being in an amusement park with family and friends. While there everyone runs to the new, thrilling roller coaster. Inevitably someone refrains from joining the others because they fear what will happen to their balance, or the consequence of perceived danger. Beyond them saying no, try to remember their face, the tightness of their body. There is no doubt that fear is an emotion based on the unknown that has an adverse physical effect.

So now that we have a different understanding of this emotion, how do we deal with it? One way is to educate yourself on possible outcomes via literature or interviewing people that have had similar experiences. Another way is pen and paper your decision. Write down the potential pros and cons of a new venture or experiences. Then think about the pros and conjure ways to defeat the cons. The key is not to put so much pressure on you. As young adults we all start a new job; there is a fear associated with that. Not only do we not know what to do. Worse, we do not know what we don't know! Yet something about the venture made us take a chance. Maybe the advancement from a starting position was endless. Maybe the salary would change your current circumstance. Whatever the reason, whether you did it consciously or unconsciously you weighed the pros and cons and used the pros as defeaters of the cons. You made a choice, regardless of the scale. You made a choice. *You faced fear.*

Another cerebral emotion that is fear based is doubt. While doubt does not invoke the physical traits of fear, I believe it is just as paralyzing. As I have stated in previous chapters, no one will deceive you as much as you. The same condition exists with doubt. While life will throw many adversaries at you, none will be harder to defeat than your own self-doubt. More times than not this lack of confidence (doubt) comes from your own past experiences. Usually a choice you made did not deliver the desired result. So the perceived shortcoming or failure of your judgment makes you untrusting. Sometimes we do not face the issue of our own lack of judgment and project this condition as not trusting others. The hard truth is, people acted as they are. You just misjudge their ability to be in sync with your choices. Unfortunately we must practice on dealing with this measure of accountability. Many people have learned to deal with self-doubt. They are called arrogant. I have been called arrogant. While I will not argue someone else's perception of me, I will explain myself to you on how I deal with doubt. I accept it. It exists. Whether you are in a leadership position or wish to be, you must learn how to face this adversary called doubt. My way of doing it is to pick a path. Period. Knowing that I believe the path I take is right. When circumstance and results prove me wrong, I make different decisions to meet goals.

So why am I arrogant when I am dealing with the same insecurities you are? I embrace there is an unknown to every decision. I accept the responsibility is mine. I do my best to prepare and put myself in a position to succeed. I am confident that I will be accountable and fix whatever goes wrong. That's the difference. You must be dedicated to your choice or path. You will remove self-doubt as that is for the cowards who are convincing themselves they are being cautious. The benefits of mastering this skill are a significant factor in attaining success of your life choices.

As we have read, every positive has its equivalent negative. Know that making good choices and having success is empowering. Hopefully you will never learn as I have that conviction is much easier than consistency! All my life I had the edge based on the fact that my life was constantly imperfect. So be it. I dealt with adversity. To quote Dale Carnegie, "When life threw lemons at me, I made lemonade." As you have success dealing with self-doubt, this positive can become a negative. As I have stated, the sword always cuts both ways. The same dedication and tactics that I used to build a twenty-million-dollar business also took it down. We will touch on this in several chapters. While there are several factors that lead to the ultimate demise, I would be disingenuous if I said self-doubt and my inability to be honest that my judgment was flawed greatly enhanced the probability of failure. Worse yet, when things continued to go wrong, self-doubt crept in. The company was in need of a new direction. Many decisions should have been made. At the time I pretended that any decision would have a great effect on clients, vendors, employees. So I stayed in a state of indecision. This would prove fatal. Worse the hypocrisy of this act was against all I stood for. For years I would teach our project managers that the only decision they could make that would anger me is *no decision*. We will address other factors in this book. Just know for now that self-doubt must be kept in check.

Know that I do not bring up this experience to be contrary to what I am writing. Quite the opposite, life is a probability, chance, change.

Not everything is going to go your way. You will make mistakes. The ones who can fix the mistakes with honest assessment wins. Had I not had consistent success I might have been able to deal with shortcomings in a more advantageous manner. I lost my edge. I allowed mounting setbacks to allow self-doubt to creep in. When that happens, you lead from a position of weakness instead of strength. Whether you are running a company or your own life, you must be able to believe that you will deal with whatever life throws at you. Liken your choice or dedication to a river. The river will encounter obstacles—pinnacles, rocks, trees. Regardless, the river goes over, under, around obstacles. The river flows. It never stops to ask why. The river stays the course. It keeps moving forward. So it is with your ability to make a decision. You must be willing to make some mistakes while you are moving forward. We all have doubt. How we deal with this is what makes or breaks us. I have been on both sides of the fence. I will take arrogant determination over doubt any day.

Another affirmation of this skill is a quote that has inspired me for a long time. Since so much time has passed I will paraphrase the quote. A reporter once asked our five-star General Patton to give a single military tactic that enabled him to have success where many failed. His answer was "It is easy. I always stayed in motion. If I stayed somewhere too long, I would be a target for the enemy. I feel as long as I am in motion, I could always change direction. Getting started when you stop is hard. Changing direction in motion is easy." As you experience life, the logic is flawless. Motivated and following this advice aided me. Losing sight of it and working contrary to it hurt me. The message is to know where you're going and to stay on your toes.

Please note that I am not suggesting you make bad choices for the sake of making a choice. What I am stating is that you must be aware of the difference of procrastinating and stagnation as opposed to studying your options diligently and choosing one. An example would be when you are purchasing a home. That is a big decision. Once that is done, you must diligently research areas, school districts, and recent sales then have a list of immediate needs for a home to provide—three-bedroom two-bath, etc.—then doing feasibility studies on your price range and affordability. This may take three to six months. Or you can make a decision to buy a home and hope someone knocks on your door with the perfect deal. My recommendation is constant education, not analysis paralysis. The act of analyzing everything to the extent that too much data clouds the mind and feeds indecision. In later chapters we will talk about honing in on a focused result. Another example would be if you were out of work. Does that really mean you're out of a job? No! When you need a job, your job for eight to ten hours a day is to look for a job. Every day you have the choice of waiting or going to get it. Bottom line, I am against waiting for your ship to come in. I recommend swimming out to get it!

After reading this chapter I would like you to put this book down for a few moments and think about the times in your life or family and friends when a decision needed to be made. So much time goes by in the process of making a decision that you or family settled into a permanent state of indecision. Rudderless. This happens so quickly that you settle in a new norm without realizing indecision brought you there. We must embrace that times change, people change, finances and the economy changes. You and I as a part of society must also adapt our choices and how we deal with adversarial consequences to our choices' intent.

This chapter has made us aware that we have not been as honest with ourselves as we thought. We must embrace that no choice leads to further inability to adapt to the changes in our life. Life flows like a river regardless. Are we going to flow with it, or will we decide to stay put as the water rushes over us? "I cannot decide" must be uncomfortable moving forward. For me it was and will be in the future a billboard sign that says you lack direction. In the future I will always have definitive *goals*!

CHAPTER 5

Goals, the Decision Maker

Show me a person that says, "I cannot decide," and I will show you a person who has no goal or dedication to his or her goal. *Webster Dictionary* defines goal as an "aim," effort to which meets an end result. I would define goals as "destination in which to focus our efforts." In both cases the goal is to achieve a desired result, which brings us to an interesting point. If life is a big game, then we must keep score. As in most games the person or team with the most goals wins. Clearly this is a metaphor for successfully accomplishing a goal, not having a lot of them at once.

This chapter will not tell you how to make goals. For that I recommend books like *Goals 101* by Gary Ryan Blair. We will discuss the emotion and the intangibles of what makes the best goal. We will discuss how the decision to make a goal will reflect on our subsequent choices. The goal for this chapter is to illustrate why goals are so important in our lives.

There are many ways to illustrate and look at goals and their impact on our choices and life. Many of us get up on a Saturday and set a goal to accomplish four domestic tasks before having dinner with family and friends. In the event we complete three out of four we are happy. To be sure these are goals. Some goals happen through natural order, like I want to graduate college in four years at age twenty-two. No denying that the accomplishment will take effort and discipline. While these two examples seem simple, they are not. The reason is many people throw the word *goal* around too often and fall short of their aim. Once this happens too many times, the proclaimer (you) of the goal begins to eradicate the word and meaning from their vocabulary. All of us, me included, set goals of being *X* amount of pounds by June. After three or four years even I do not take myself seriously. So to start, let's try to hold this word in reverent respect to our desires. All other ends will be our *aim*. Goals are serious business.

I believe it is important to give this word added respect because not only will it shape your life but also this word will make your choices. So when we say that "we set a goal," it should be something that is going to profoundly shape your life for the better. We are all at different stages and have different needs in life. So when you make a goal, it must be deeply personal. While many can juggle many goals at once, my experience of one at a time can be highly effective. Again having a goal takes thinking, studying, planning, changing environment and routines. This is serious stuff. The benefits are that our choices will seem easier and fall in line with the vision of our life.

All of us have used this word irresponsibly and fallen short. Before setting new goals we must acknowledge what went wrong in the past with the use of the word and how we applied it to our life. After dissecting shortcomings and success on past goals I am willing to bet that the only factor of success and failure was *desire*. Desire is often used as noun (idea), as some wish that is made. Most will use it as an adjective (description) to describe their feeling of longing for an item or situation. The truth is when understood and used properly, this word is a verb (action!) The word is meant to imply your ability to do whatever it takes to meet a goal. Wanting and needing are nice. When you really want something, when you want to achieve it, your desire will make the goal for you. Henceforth, this should set your goals from here on out. Desire for a specific end will compel you to live your desire. All other wants and needs are aims.

Many in the business world as in life like to set sales goals, earnings goals, and market share goals. Certainly worthy. The stock market keeps score this way. Achieving goals is the desire. Think of your goal as the brain in the body. Then desire is heart. Choice then becomes your air. Breathing. All three are separate but need one another. This metaphor goes one step further. After the brain sets the goal and the heart pumps it to life. We rely on the air we breathe (choice) to keep it going. Now we just have to be careful of the air we breathe. Can we actually live our goals? I would argue there is no other way.

Dianne was in a rut. At thirty-one she had been vice president of her bank for the past two years. She accomplished this only four years after getting her master's. Diane had ambition, focus, and a great sense of humor. What she lacked was discipline in the rest of her life. Working sixty to seventy hours a week left her little time for socializing outside her family let alone meeting her own domestic demands in living alone. Diane wanted to make some changes but it never came together for her. So in two short years she gained fifteen additional pounds and found herself filling even more time at work and with family. In her inability to acknowledge change, her weight gain began to work on her psyche. When dates did not work out, she wondered if it was her or her added weight.

Despite all her success in other areas of her life, self-doubt found its way to her. This self-doubt made her hide in safe places, work and family. Worse her best friend from college called to say she would be getting married in sixteen short months. Being intelligent and giving herself time to reflect she identified changes she would like to make. So she applied the same concept that enabled her to reach vice president in four years. She set a goal that if followed would enable her to make the necessary changes. She set a goal for losing twenty pounds by the wedding. Her desire to meet that goal forced the following choices to attain it.

For the next sixteen months she woke an hour early to do cardio exercise and think about her day while doing it. She made her own lunch to ensure a consistent diet and ate at her desk. Four nights a week she worked out with weights to ensure a better shape. Diane changed her schedule with family and friends to alternate with Saturday nights and Sundays. After six months she found that she was sharper in her thinking and focused more on everything she did. Nothing was taken for granted. Work was routine, but fitting in this new lifestyle took work as well. So making the time to have it all became her obsession. By the wedding she had accomplished her goals and took a guy she had been dating the last four months. I suspect her confidence rose and this new suitor gravitated toward her strengths.

Along the way Diane began to make choices in line with her goal. She needed time at the gym. So she decided to do reports on Saturday mornings in lieu of being with friends. Rather than working seventy hours she decided to trust coworkers with tasks and learned to be a better delegator than doer. Diane enlisted the cooperation of family in her desire to find more balance so they would be understanding of her absence a couple of times a month. More than anything she never strayed from the path. When decisions (choices) were to be made, Diane deferred to the choice that best suited her goals. Her desire demanded she lived her goal. No one, not even her, was surprised she did it.

While Diane and the circumstances are fictitious, the scenario and results are real. All of us have something we want. Remember, it is not worthy of a goal until the desire compels us to make one. The intangibles of this endeavor are endless because you must make choices to complete it. There is a time frame, so there are consequences. You are living an imperfect life, so you will get plenty of practice to adjusting your choices to suit your goal. Holding yourself accountable to your goal will enable your self-respect to soar. Most of all people will see the best in you.

People seeing the best in you are what I love most. You do not set goals for others. You do it for you. Afterward, whether they are aware of the goal or not, people respond to your strength and confidence. You begin to be admired!

Our own life experience was set in motion by maintaining goals. "Make a life to be on your own at sixteen, get a two-bedroom apartment at nineteen. Buy a home by twenty-five. Open a business by thirty. Be able to retire at forty." Sounds crazy?

It was and I did it! Probably the best analogy I could give is imagining you're on a highway and you're sixty miles from your destination. Traffic is not moving. Your goal is to still get there on time, so rather than giving up and saying that you're going to be late, you get off the next exit and take the long route but you stay moving and get there quicker. That's what being around me from 1996 to 2010 would have been like, focused on goals. The goals never ended, yearly goals, monthly goals, weekly goals, daily goals.

When our daughter made it in to the college of her choice, my wife and I were ecstatic. Our daughter going to college was nice enough. But from where my wife and I started to our daughter setting a goal in freshman year and accomplishing it, what a natural high. I am beaming remembering that feeling. So to review, college was in order, house was leverage to 15 percent of its value. Our real estate holdings were leveraged at 38 percent of their values. So we purchased a two-bedroom condo for our daughter to use during college, and we would continue renting when she was done. So essentially we made one more goal. There are many reasons for making a goal. Just know that this goal as all others were backed by desire. We set a goal to have 250,000 in personal cash to invest, have no debt in the construction company, and attain one more property to ensure the real estate equity would be over three million. We set this goal to accomplish it in three years, 2010. I would be forty that year. The goal was to establish 100,000 a year in passive income. For those that do not know what that means. That means your assets earn that money, not my efforts that earned income. My wife and I had the skills and systems in place to do it. All we had to do was stay on track.

In the three years from 2008 to 2010 many things happened to knock us off our goal. In 2008 there began a severe recession in our economy. Presidents had changed in 2009 and Congress in 2010. Financial regulations completely changed. Despite banking, real estate, and my clients changing their desire to grow, we stayed on the message regardless of roads taken and hit every one of our goals in June 2010. Our son would go off to college that year as well. All our married life we set goals and met every one of them. Throughout the process there were ups and downs. Our love for one another and our mutual desires and plans enabled us to live the life we envisioned, and our respect for one another was the glue that kept it together. So now what?

We were together twenty-two years and raised our family and accomplished all our goals. Now what? Stick to the plan? Sell off my company and make new goals?

Looking back this is where the business went wrong and our life was compromised. I decided to do nothing. After working eighty hours a week I would enjoy life a little. I allowed my employees to run things as they were well taught through experience and the classes I had given. The decision was not to put pressure on me to have goals. I gave goals for my employees. This proved worthless as there was not any true desire, nor did I deliver consequences. Worse I was dragged back in hard as the economy came full circle and we wound up suing for 2.6 million in receivable from April 2011 to September of 2013. All choices made were Band-Aids or reactions to circumstances. There was no plan in place. No goals. So I just went into default behavior and worked. Trouble was, even though I worked every day fifteen to sixteen hours a day, I was working plugging holes. No one was steering the ship and we ran aground one too many times.

Most people would blame the economy, the legal system, the process of construction, and the lack of rights a contractor has. I knew it was me, but after so much success, I could not see why. After the dust settles you can see that goals always aided in my choices. Having no goals, my choices were not consistent enough to inspire employees and clients. Everyone knew something was missing. I had to be honest, my desire was not passionate enough to make goals. I did what General Patton said never to do. I stayed put then got run over.

No goals led to few consistent choices. Failed choices meant more aimless choices. This allowed self-doubt to creep in, and then shock and no decision to correct. So all we worked for in twenty-two years was gone in three. All I could hear was my grandfather's words as a child, "Just when you think you're in, you're out! A measure of complacency had settled in. To use our road analogy, when I got off the exit to search a better way, I had no real destination to focus on and stayed lost. Had I had a goal, I would have dealt with the adversity in a manner of what my goals dictated. Choice.

In conclusion I will never forget how important a goal is to act as a compass in my life. Goals keep you focused on where you are going. Choices are easy to make as long as you do not lose sight of your goal. What do you desire? Set your mind to it! Allow your choices to meet this obsession to take precedence in your life. Know if you cannot make a decision, it is due to a lack of goal. Learn from my mistake and find one. Your future does depend on this.

CHAPTER 6

Choosing the Consequences

"My house is upside down" (owe more than it is worth). This was a common cry from 2007 to 2011. Many people either bought too high or overleveraged their purchase. Most gave up their homes and walked away. Some filed bankruptcy. Still some dealt with the loss and continued to pay the monthly mortgage. Sad story? True, a series of miscalculation had brought bad fortune. Most had no idea the housing market would crash. What is important for us to realize when life delivers a surprise punch and knocks us down? The fight is not over. At the lowest times of our lives we still have choices.

To me the lowest we can be as human beings is to feel there is no chance to achieve a desired outcome. No hope. Just thinking about a loved one saying they are terminally ill. Sometimes circumstances of life alter your course. During these times we must be more keenly aware of the consequences of our choices. *You are not your circumstances that befall your life. You are the consequences that you chose to deal with the circumstances.*

Tragically the examples above deal with the matter of this chapter. The people described above had to make choices to deal with their circumstance. This chapter is for those that do not realize their goals and choices sometimes have unintended consequences that can be dealt with before it results to hopelessness.

In chapter 2 we had discussed cause and effect. We discussed how our choices (cause) played a part in the effect (outcome). My hope in this chapter is to illustrate that when we deny, hide, or run from consequences, again this conscience choice brings more consequence. Even good choices bring unintended bad consequences. So the point is to recognize your role and act accordingly.

In chapter 3 we discussed how to deal with our choices through honesty, which is accountability. In chapter 4 we discussed that "I cannot decide" is a lack of choice through past consequences or perceived consequences. We must change our attitude if we are going to live the life we choose. The life you choose is your possession; the consequences you face are the payment. Know that you get to choose the method of payment.

Growing up in the Bronx in the seventies and eighties, it was not uncommon for most people to feel they were a victim of circumstance. We grew up very blue collar. You went to work; you did your best, paid your bills, and hoped nothing went wrong. When something did go wrong, it was either someone else's fault or some mysterious act of nature. For the Italians reading the book, you will understand this condition as "Eh! What are you going to do?" As if they had no control over the outcome or the consequences. To enable yourself to feel this way is to believe you have no control over your life, which I would say is no life at all. In this social environment there is an extreme lack of accountability for consequences.

I mention this as a matter to assimilate your own social condition to understand this chapter. To put it plainly you will suffer consequences whether you act or you don't. The difference is being aware that we have to deal with consequences whether through our own actions, or the actions of those we surround ourselves with. After reading this book there will be consequences for the choices you make to live the life you want. The trick is to be ready to accept them and stick to your goals. As a result of your choices whether through adversity or progress, consequences will follow. Although there are no guarantees, at least you are living in a manner that you choose. I submit it is a lot easier to react to consequences when you control the outcome than when you do not.

My friend Gary passed away due to a massive heart failure at the age of forty-two. Gary left behind a wife and two children ages fourteen and five respectively at the time. At the time of his passing Gary was 70 percent of his household income, as well as being the emotional support of his wife who had been taking on the majority of the children's day-to-day activity. For the married couples in our culture, you can describe the lifestyle as normal.

Gary's wife Theresa went through a bereavement process. The shock of losing her husband in a second before her eyes, as witnessed by her kids, would put anyone in shock. Be mindful that no one wants to prepare for these circumstances nonetheless live them.

Unfortunately in one second she was a single parent, head of household, sole supporter, mother and father.

Consider, whether she made a choice or not, consequences would follow. Whether she made the right choices or not, consequences would follow. Just the thought of that mind-set is suffocating. Worse, regardless of moral support, her choices and subsequent consequences would affect her and her children only. That is loneliness that people sitting in your living room cannot take away.

As a consequence of Gary's unusual passing Theresa had her back against the wall. Instinct and survival kicked in and she took steps to ensure she would not lose her house. She then took steps to ensure her children continued with their current school schedule and financing. Going at alone in this endeavor is one thing. Knowing everyone is watching you, analyzing you, critiquing you, that is quite another matter. As much as I wanted to assist, there was very little that I could do. So I reminded Theresa that decisions, choices, must be made and stuck to regardless of pressure from family. Due to her ability to deal with adversity and all the unintended consequences that she never considered as she made a go at it alone, Theresa has my respect, not only for doing a great job, but also the grace she showed in doing it. Theresa persevered despite not having her own family available as they stayed in Poland. I guess that I should not have been surprised as she had made the choice to make a life here without the benefit of family support.

Tragically many households every year suffer a similar fate. Many are not handled with the love and grace that Theresa showed. So how is it that people without adversity are unable to acknowledge and deal with consequences? How is it that people endure a subpar standard of living and the consequences without making proactive choices to handle the outcome? Using common sense described in the situations illustrated in this chapter we know that consequences follow regardless of choices. We know that even in the most hopeless situations we still have the ability to choose. So why do we accept circumstances that beget more adversarial consequences? That answer is personal to you. All I can say is if you are going to choose the life you want, know that there are going to be consequences. Better that you're in control over at least part of the outcome.

Socrates has been quoted as saying, "The secret is to put all your energy not on the old but building the new." Circumstances change—sometimes these are not in your control. You are always able to choose to what extent it affects your life by being aware that consequences, good and bad, will come. Better that you are aware of the consequences and choose the one that least affects your goals.

All of us reading this book can think of one thing that blindsided us and changed the course of your life. Some of us were not aware at the time that we still controlled our destiny. It's possible that we just took life one day at a time and just rolled with the punches. Not anymore. For it is at this juncture that you must be aware that all is not lost. Tough times do not last. Tough people do. Circumstances do not define you. Your choices and the consequences you choose to deal with do.

One of the main motivations for writing this book revolved around this chapter. Sadly, I do not believe tragic circumstances like death in the family, losing your job, prison, illness define any person's life. I believe choosing to be a victim is the more permanent definition. My hope is through reading this book your subconscious will trigger the inner fire to recognize that choices that will define your life must be made. As in most situations in life, it will not be easy. The author wishes to represent that the consequences that you choose to deal with the circumstance will make it tolerable.

Worth reminding the reader one more time, "You cannot control circumstances. You can control the consequences to deal with the circumstance."

CHAPTER 7

Environment, Education, and Culture

Many people reading this book will discount their bad decisions based on the author not understanding the environment or culture that they came from as to why their choices had such dire consequences. First, let's address this overused word of *understanding*. Stop bullshitting yourself. When speaking of your own life, it does not need to be understood. Merely accepted or not accepted. Many people who state "they do not understand" are merely glazing over that they do not accept the reality. You understand the language; you understand the law or the customs. You may not like them or accept them. Acknowledging this will go a long way to putting your life and this chapter into perspective.

All of us grow up in a cultural environment. Whether that culture is borne of your ethnic, religious, or economic background. These factors shaped the culture you were raised in. All three may shape some of your cultures. What is important is that you acknowledge that your prior perspective in making choices was not thought of in a cognitive sense. You made the choices in line with a level of comfort with your culture. Sadly many of us come from different levels of dysfunction due to our culture and the ever-changing world.

To give a somewhat recent well-known example of a culture clash, most are familiar with the choices made by Michael Vick, the professional football player. Michael was a superior athlete raised in a poverty-stricken area of Newport News, Virginia. In his community, dog fighting, cock fighting, as well as other nefarious practices, were commonplace. Michael used his athletic prowess to gain a scholarship in the local Virginia Tech, taking his team to be undefeated in his first year as a starter. This put him on the national stage and was rewarded two years later with a sixty-two-million-dollar contract from the Falcons as a first-round draft pick.

Michael Vick was living in a different world from where he came just four short years before. While he should receive respect and compensation for the choices he made to get there, again the sword always cut both ways.

In an effort to keep ties to his roots as well as have a vehicle for some less fortunate family members, Michael Vick engaged in an activity that was legally wrong but culturally accepted. Michael Vick funded and participated in all ways of dog fighting. Worse due to his celebrity status and the perceived public respect for his athletic prowess, he lied. He did not feel his "minor law infraction" would affect him. We know the rest of the story. He went to jail, paid millions in fines, was removed from his contract with the NFL, and forced into bankruptcy due to his mounting debts.

To be clear I found his choices and actions to be deplorable. I thought the consequences were fitting. I will also state that the way he has dealt with his consequences is worthy of respect. Having said that I could not help but assimilate my life to his and the choices that I could have made.

For instance, where I grew up in the Bronx, gambling was everywhere. From betting the "numbers," the last three digits of a racetrack total payouts, gambling in every sport, as well as legal gambling in lotto and offtrack betting. Just know that it was in every living room, kitchen, coffee shop, jobsites, clubs—everywhere. We all knew it was illegal, but that would have been like telling me that so was watching TV. I was going to do it anyway. I did. Not only did I bet but also I worked within the circles to take and pay and collect gambling debts. The fact that it was illegal was of no consequence.

My family and friends did it, so did their parents. For generations this was commonplace. It was part of our culture.

So when I moved to Jersey, I had clients; I had the capital and the know-how to engage in this cultural rite. Wrong! I was in a different place, which meant comfortable choices would bring uncomfortable consequences. I also had a family that would live those consequences. Michael Vick had a career, family, team, and league that would live his consequences. What does all this mean? Both Michael and I have had the opportunity to reflect on how our culture makes and shapes our decisions. Could Michael have argued, "You do not understand our culture." Maybe, but no one would accept it! Get it?

Be mindful, there are many positive advantages of many cultures. The purpose of this chapter is to acknowledge our past environment and how it fits with our desired future. Do not make choices until you answer this question. There are many stigmatism in each culture that shape how we first see the world and how we now see it the further we get from our beginnings.

Many reading this book have or have had aspirations of moving somewhere beautiful that they desired growing up. Then you get older; you marry. It is then that you yearn for your children to be part of your extended family. So you make choices to compromise and live elsewhere to please all. Some may be in an environment where there is a generational family business. That is the culture of your family. You have been living it since a child, discussing it, and respond to the responsibilities of it. Maybe the religious culture is so stringent that you cannot imagine life outside the culture you were raised.

The point I am trying to make is we all have reasons for the life decisions we have made. We do not need to understand. You and I have to accept that it was your choice! As it was then. And it is in the future. You may have felt like a victim of circumstance. You're not!

Growing up in the Bronx is not a culture of advancement. Of course I am stereotyping, as not all conform to the culture. I certainly did not. In the eighties you were expected to suffer through high school, get a diploma, and get a job. In the event that you excelled through natural ability at school and received a college scholarship,

"Why not try college." No one discussed degrees. No one discussed entrepreneurship. Conversely, there was plenty of discussion of giving up your individuality to join a local union or a civil service. Bottom line, we were taught success is for the lucky, not for us.

The culture and environment was do not get in trouble, get a job, and work hard. In the event all falls perfectly, you may be able to own a car and buy a house. Sadder still, in other cultures, in the city the expectation was to find the fastest route to social assistance. Unwittingly giving up your freedom to make all sorts of choices.

While some reading this book can state a hundred people they know that overcame this environment, I am writing this book because I know that there are hundreds of thousands who did not. Consider this. Even today in the new millennium, there are generations of people in the city who have not left the city limits. Imagine that? How much do their environment shape their choices? Sure they see a different world on TV, but that is just the stuff on TV. Where they reside, that is life. People's perception is their reality. So whether you're stuck in a lower economic environment or a strict religious environment, your education and ability to make better choices is limited. Note with benefit that I am not saying working a union or civil servant job is not a good life. It is. I mention this to note that there are still a great many choices and paths. In my environment, only the easy ones were possible.

We must acknowledge that society has produced many contributors from less than optimum environments. Do they possess more intelligence and physical gifts than you and I? In a very small percentage the answer is yes. Most that do make it to live a life far better than the environment offered them understood their culture, but they did not accept it! So again note, stop misusing this word. It is not important to understand. Merely accept it, or do not.

I did not accept what a culture and environment expected of me. I envisioned more. Having an eleventh-grade education and a young family that was dependent on my ability to earn the social outlook was grim. As you can tell by reading this book, the ideas are common sense, but the way I view it and illustrate them is unique. So as with anyone making life choices you have to be practical and honest about where you are in life. No skill, no education, and responsibilities that a thirty-year-old can barely manage at the age eighteen. Suffocating! Like many others in my position, I recognize what very few do. The rich live in fear of being middle class; the middle class live in fear of being poor. Me, I had nothing to lose! Who cares if I tried and failed? That was expected anyway, right? There is something very liberating about everyone expecting you to fail. The worst thing that could happen is you prove everyone right. Ever think about making choices to prove everyone wrong? You can.

You can because we all have the choice to live the life we choose. As illustrated in this chapter our environment and culture if dealt with honestly have a substantial impact on the way we view the world and the choices we can assess. The author believes that education solves these social ills. Does our education predetermine our destiny? Does education limit our goals? As you read this, in this very moment, yes. The good news, we live in a society where education in every form is available at our fingertips. Any choice you make from this point on can and should be ascertained after educating yourself in the matter. Whether you are making a career choice, a change of location, a social or religious change. You can educate yourself in the matter. Moreover you can do it thirty minutes a day for two weeks.

On the subject of education I believe that many school systems fail at teaching children life skills like the ability to make comprehensive choices after reviewing cause and effect. The good news is that as in pre-revolutionary to today, anyone can educate themselves if they choose. Let's take a moment to analyze this word. *Educate* is from the Latin root word *educu*, which means "to draw out," so using the suffix *tion* or act of, *education* really means the act of drawing out what is within you! Imagine that. We have been led to believe that education is putting information in. Books, computers, personal testimony are the stimulus. The education is you. While I had no formal education, my wanting to learn never ceased. You are the choices you make. I had decided to be a builder, a real one. Be a builder that could lead and teach a hundred men to work in concert. So I needed to learn, and fast. My decision was to take jobs for the next ten years to learn, not earn. I would do side jobs for the earning. Learning would be paramount. I utilized my time wisely, spending hours on a job after all had left to study what had been done one trade at a time. Then I would study how the text I was reading related to the task I was undertaking. Back then and now I kept an open mind and interrogated anyone that could impart knowledge. I was always very fond of saying during this period that "I would not take a shit without having a trade book in my hand." My choice was to educate my way toward my goals. No different than a young adult I went to school on my chosen path. Anyone can do this.

Many people will make attempts to blame a school, teacher, or parent. What is your excuse today?

Education is not holding you back. Your desire to draw out and draw upon that which inspires you is holding you back. True, you may not know all you need to make a choice to set a goal, but you are a choice away from being on the right path. The only wrong choice you can make is to do nothing. Do not think of education as something you lack. Rather think of it as something inside you waiting to be discovered. You bought this book. So something is burning inside you for a different life. Ironically I have discovered the way to learning is to be childlike. A child sees everything as amazing. A child sees no limits, only possibilities. A child has no social ego. All they have is a wondrous curiosity. How much can you learn right now living that way for one week?

Reacquaint yourself with the culture and environment of your upbringing. How did your culture take part in your decisions? Reevaluate your feelings on education and how your beliefs in your ability shaped your choices. Recognize that you cannot have a different life if you are not willing to see outside your culture that may be holding you back. Make choices toward the life you choose, not the culture and environment you believe has defined you. Understand?

CHAPTER 8

God's Will, Destiny, and Other Esoteric Factors

"I will leave it in God's hands."

"My destiny will be revealed to me."

"My right hand is itchy so I will be lucky at the casino."

We have all made or heard such statements in the past. Are we wrong to feel that way? Did you really go to the casino because your hand itched? Did you not apply to the colleges or your choice because destiny would show you the way? Will God orchestrate all things to ensure your desired result?

Many are already answering, "Whatever happens, it is meant to be," "No one knows Gods plan," "Everything happens for a reason." While all the statements are familiar. They are a complete departure from the mind-set of this book.

Many miracles happen every day that are documented. Some miracles have their own book or movie. In the author's objective opinion, I too have faith in the possibilities of miracles. Unfortunately the book is on choice and not faith. So where does that leave our choices, consequences, and God's will? Where is the line? At what point do you take ownership of your life? Good things happen to us all. So do tragic things. Can you honestly state you know what is destiny and what is choice?

In this chapter we will approach this very controversial topic. The book is about giving you the social awareness to take ownership of choosing the life you want. While I do not have concrete answers for every scenario in life, I may be able to provide an interesting perspective on how to rationalize your experiences and emotions in dealing with life, fate, and choices.

In the spirit of being honest, know that I was raised Catholic. While I am very spiritual, I do not believe in orthodoxy, so I do not profess or advocate any religion over the other. All religions have something positive and wonderful for the believer as they are meant to inspire the believer to a higher thought and life. Since age sixteen I have studied theology. Theology offers the student not only the study of religion but of history and sociology as well. I state this so you may view my perspective on this matter in the proper light. The rest of the chapter I may use the words that I am familiar with like God or Creator. Remember, the book is on choice, and in this chapter we must address where the Creator lies in those choices and consequences. While my opinions may seem strong, they are strong in relation to the context of this book.

Why do bad things happen to good people? How do we justify a child dying of an accident or cancer? What about the couple who has lived their life according to their faith yet is unable to have children. Is this the will of the Creator?? Many poor drug addicts and alcoholics have won the lottery. Why have many less than moral men and women risen to fortune and fame? While we mourned for our country on 9/11/2001, many in other parts of the world were celebrating "God's will." So why do bad things happen to some good people? Conversely, if there is a moral Creator deciding the fate of the righteous and wicked, then why are less than moral people rewarded with riches?

All of us have had the same thoughts. All of us have asked *why*. Some people have lost their faith answering these questions. Some have surrendered the gift of life to support their belief that it is, in fact, all God's will. Many reading this book are parents who will have to attempt to answer these difficult, complex questions to their children. How do we approach this complex issue without feeling hopeless? Where do our choices fall in line with the power of the Creator? Below is my perspective as explained to my children in their twenties.

First off, I believe in a God of immense unquantifiable love. Just spend three hours anywhere in silence and be amazed at the plants, trees, people, structures, birds, dogs, the clouds, sun, stars. The awesome power of creation and life is made of love, certainly nothing evil. The gift of life is a wonderful sight to see, when you are open to seeing other life besides your own. Conversely, I do not believe in a Creator with so much love that can be vengeful and judgmental to the life it has created. Rather than review thirty years of study on the matter, just accept that God did not make man in his image. Rather, man in all periods and places continually make a God in their image. For the purpose of this analogy, let's assume I am correct in saying that the Creator is Love. Period.

All of us have parents, or are parents. We are the creator of our children's life. Like the Creator of this world, we love what we created. We give our children guidance and principles. Moreover, what we really work toward when it comes to our children is to give them a life of their (you got it!) choice. We want our children to be happy. The best way to be happy is to live the life you choose. So it is with a Creator. I believe we are all God's children. Through God's love we were given life! No more, no less. Through this divine love he has given us the right to choose how we respect the gifts given. You are not going to make all the right choices; neither will your children. I guarantee, no matter how bad your children screw up, you will love them and try to help them make better choices. That is what creating out of love does.

Imagine you had the power to create a whole universe. Imagine you had the power to create billions of living things that need one another. Imagine you had dominion over all you have created. Would you spend the rest of your time watching, judging, interfering in the lives of the people and animals you created? Of course not, your love and creative power would give the same rationale that one parent has for one child as the creator has for seven billion people. You cannot prepare your child for every choice in life. You wish for the best and love them unconditionally. You cannot control all the situations, danger, and harm that are prevalent in the world we are sharing with other people's choices. All you can do is pray that all works out okay and show gratitude along the way. As much as we create their life, your children's life is not yours. It is theirs, and you are going to love them anyway.

So if creation is love and free will, where does faith come in? All monotheist religions as well as other faiths have a strong belief in the afterlife. Most teach that our souls have existed before in another time or consciousness. While there is proof on both sides, the possibility of our continuing existence is salvation for this life as in the next. Profoundly I believe that we all have a short time on this earth to find divinity in ourselves. Regardless of your culture, or religion, we all have the gift of life to experience. Faith and religion give us ideas and a format to discover the hidden gifts of life with the promise that the end here on earth is not the end of our existence. Due to my faith in this belief, I do not mourn tragedy. I believe in the power of creation. God does not stand in judgment of you. In the event you missed the intended lessons due to tragedy, you will not be cheated, but given another chance. This objective is worthy of any faith.

Now here we are trying to do our best to respect the gift of life endowed by the Creator and our parents. Do we give up the gift of choice? Do we leave everything to fate? Of course not. Your parents did not get you arrested for drinking and driving. Your choices did. Where does God end and your choices begin? For instance, we have all watched a sporting event where the triumphant athlete gives all the credit to God. Well, where was God the first ten years of your career? Does God really favor you more than the team you beat? How about the losing team? When they lose they talk about more practice, more dedication. Then when they finally win they thank God. I am fine with thanking God for everything. I am not okay with you holding him accountable. You are!

We are all given the gift of life. In America we are given the gift of freedom to live the life endowed by the Creator. Not even God can guarantee happiness. The pursuit of happiness is guaranteed. That is life. Therefore, if we live our life with respect to the creative process, then our choices would be more in line with gratitude instead of greed and avarice. Now that I have explained my beliefs as to where God lies in the outcome of our lives, let's get back to choice.

Many humble, intuitive learned people and prophets ask God for guidance, perfectly acceptable. Conversely to ask for and expect a result is in no way in line with the gifts you were given. For instance, I would teach my children to fish so they can eat. Even if they prayed for a fish, I would probably give them bait. God does not decide whether you eat well. The Creator has given us the metabolism to feed off the plants and animals of the world. No go out and catch your own fish. You have been given the arms, legs, and mind to out-maneuver most other living things. When you do not, is it God's will?

Bottom line is you own your choices. Not God. Clearly if you are a person of faith, it would be reasonable to feel a higher power is guiding your steps. My book just illustrates that God can help guide your steps. Just make sure you are walking where you choose. Faith is a great inspiration and motivation. I use it. After I make a goal, then it is okay to ask for help. Just remember that God helps those that help themselves.

The issue with leaning on God for results instead of guidance is simply this. You cannot hold God accountable. Not because he does not exist in the physical form. No! You cannot hold him accountable because it was your choice, not his. Your life, your journey, your choices, your results. Period. God is no more to blame for a horrible accident than your parents are to blame for not living the life you envisioned. We are all trying to do the best we can on this little blue marble. Do not make it more difficult than it is. Using God as a decision maker and scorekeeper is not what any loving parent would want for their child. Certainly not the relationship you would want with God. Conversely you should find ways to serve him, not the other way around. Be careful what you pray for. You just might get it.

Making choices in life is very important. You will use many factors to make your choices in life. Whether your religious beliefs, your expectations of family members, or economic reasons, whatever the factors are. The factors are not as important as you owning the choice and owning the consequences of your choice. Do not surrender your desires and actions to superstitions and destiny. You choose your destiny as well. No doubt circumstances will manifest themselves to illuminate your destiny. In the end you will see that your thoughts, desires, and choices led you to your destiny.

Have faith that if you believe you're accountable for your choices and actions, you will be able to live the life you choose. Pray for the guidance, patience, and strength to continue the journey you chose. You will live the consequences. Have faith that if you live in accordance with becoming a better person, you are paying respect to your parents and the Creator. When things go wrong as it often will, know that it is life. We have been given the greatest gifts above all living things on earth. We were given the ability to choose. Choose our religion, choose our destination, choose a partner to love, choose a point of view. Using those gifts to the fullest is all you would ask of your children. I suspect that is all God would ever ask of you.

CHAPTER 9

"I Had No Choice"

The psychological surrender of these words is just as disturbing as really having no choice. Clearly life throws curveballs at us all. We all have survival instincts and use them to prioritize when we encounter adversity. By feeling these priorities so strongly, we believe we have no choice but to make choices in line with our first priorities. This type of adversity allows us to really evaluate what is important.

In this chapter we will redefine what "I had no choice" means. More importantly we will remove the victim line of thinking and replace it with a more positive line of thinking. We can do this as we are more than halfway through with this book, and we recognize that while we cannot control all circumstances, we can control the consequences. We can make and own tough choices.

There is no magic cure. In taking the risk to live the life you choose, you will be exposed to the punch in the belly. You will encounter an event that you did not see coming that changes your life, your goals, your priorities. These words will cross your mind. The only difference will be you will have renewed confidence that you always have choices.

Can you remember the last time you made a choice under the hopeless term of "I had no choice"? As some time has gone by, do you still feel that way? Were your options really limited, or was your belief in yourself limited? What were the factors that led to your choices and decisions? Did you make decisions to survive or save face with a perceived norm? Now that the ordeal has been dealt with, would you make different choices? Let's look at a scenario that many can relate to and input our own values to this scenario.

Patrick was a thirty-three-year-old civil engineer working in NYC. Patrick and his wife Lisa have been married for eight years and have a six-year-old boy Joseph and four-year-old daughter Jackie. Patrick loved his $90,000 a year job, and Lisa worked part-time three days a week for a family member who owned a restaurant. Although they managed the mortgage on their new home the past three years, saving was tough as a growing family always has household concerns to deal with. What made life problematic was Jackie was diagnosed with kidney illness and needed dialysis. Most months there was just enough to make the bills and fill the two financed cars with gas.

In late November Patrick was told that the firm was going to have to close due to lack of payments from clients. One week earlier Lisa was told that she would only be needed one day a week as sales have been dropping month after month. The news Patrick had to share with his wife was devastating. They were barely keeping up with bills bringing in $6,500 per month. Now with unemployment, and Lisa working one day a week, they would only have $2,900 a month to work with. Knowing that there was no savings, Patrick could not shake that feeling in his stomach, as if he just had received a punch.

Patrick spent the next three days trying to answer the "why me?" then started making calls to college buddies and associates hoping to land an interview. Christmas was only weeks away. He knew the chances of hiring were slim to none. What was he going to do? The kids were looking forward to Christmas, the winter was coming, and oil for the house was already very expensive. What was going to happen to their perfect credit? Now he would have to listen to his and Lisa's parents saying that the house and payments were too much of a stretch. Worse, the pressure made him feel they were right.

At this juncture, just about any choice he would make could have been justified as "I had no choice." Some have known the loneliness and despair of being in this position. In the event you cannot empathize, then sympathize and try to imagine being there. No matter what choice you make, someone is compromised. There is no getting out of this situation without there being casualties.

One week letter he received his Cobra letter for medical insurance from his now closed firm. The company had been paying $1,400 per month for insurance and now he would have to pay it. Being his daughter had a kidney disease, he could not live without it. That would mean he would be left with $1,500 to pay $700 in utilities, $2,500 for mortgage, interest, insurance as well as $800 in car payments for the two cars on top of the $200 per month for car insurance. Between Lisa and Patrick's credit cards the $9,000 in debt was $600 a month in minimums. Without buying any food or filling up the cars with gas, Patrick was $3,300 a month short of meeting expenses. Without finding a job in the next sixty days there was no way to make it. At this point he could have robbed a bank and state with confidence he had no choice. At least not the choices he wanted to face.

Can you see what I see? "I had no choice" really means that I cannot win. No matter what direction I go, I lose. The truth is, Patrick is right. So is everyone else in this scenario. Not that they had no choice. They cannot avoid dire consequences to the unforeseen circumstance. They cannot win. You're going to lose the battle. In that event, let's focus on winning the war.

Patrick will survive this. The good news is he gets to choose the consequences—default on credit cards, default on car loans, default on mortgage or all. Not pretty. Very painful, but he still had a choice. Patrick did something few do in this scenario. He focused on his daughter's health care, made deals with the credit card and car companies to give him the next four months to regroup, and put his house up for sale. Patrick knew that the past and present were irrevocable. He was honest with himself and realized that he could not win. In being honest about his present, Patrick focused on his future. Patrick worked with the firm's old clients on a consultant fee and opened his own company two years later. Patrick was determined to be a victor. Lisa, Joseph, and Jackie needed his best, and he would give it.

Through no honesty and rational thinking, Patrick admitted temporary defeat. Patrick would not let this setback define him. Priorities and a desire to succeed for his family forced him to make goals. From the despair of "I had no choice," Patrick found his voice. Feeling like a victim was not for him. He lost his home he had hoped to raise his family in, Lisa lost a car, and their perfect credit was destroyed. Fortunately for Patrick he had no time to dwell on his losses as he was busy building a more perfect future. Patrick chose the consequences. Once the choice was made, he no longer felt like a victim. In fact he was proud to sell the house and start a new upward climb to better credit every month.

By using the example above I have tried to use a middle-of-the-road relatable scenario. I am sure anyone can come up with worse circumstances. The point is 99 percent of the time you can choose the consequences. "I had no choice" does not mean that literally. Honesty must lead you to the conclusion that you simply cannot win. As illustrated above, you always have your future. Do not give up a moment of the present thinking about the past.

Patrick was wiser than me. To be honest it took me about two years and 1.5 million of leveraged and hard cash to realize that I could not win. As you have read, I was a hardworking successful guy with no fear. So when the real estate market tanked, I had no choice, had to pay the mortgages in spite of tenants not paying rent. When three of the top ten retailers in the country stopped paying their bills, I had to pay the subs. I had no choice. When medical, general liability, and umbrella policies went up 60 percent in the two-year period, I said I have to pay it. I have no choice! The psychological surrender of repeating those words and not being honest did uncorrectable harm. When I was saying I had no choice, I really thought it was temporary. Tough times don't last; tough people do. I still believe that. Now I would add if tough people do not make tough choices, they won't last.

You are going to begin to choose the life you want. The future you envision. There will be circumstances beyond your control that may make you delay your journey. Through redefining the phrase "I have no choice" we are better prepared to attack this hopeless phrase with clarity. The first is to be honest that something about the plan is flawed. Of course you did not anticipate the circumstance, but what happens once will happen again. How we alter our life and plan to prepare for this revealed condition will define us.

The second is to realize you lost temporarily and must focus harder on making choices for your future to meet goals. Lastly, recognize that you have no time to be a victim. As a victim you will bring greater despair than the consequences.

In the past eight chapters we have acknowledged the importance of choice. We have learned the skill set of analyzing our choices. Together we studied the intrinsic values and principles to form new choices. This book has brought to light the dangers of not making a choice, to the illumination of the beneficial relationship with goals and choices. Lastly, we learned how to embrace the environment that shapes our choices, the ability to understand the choices we make with our back against the wall, all in an effort to make better choices in the future. For the next five chapters I will assume you are ready to start the day-by-day quest to choose the life you want. At this point we are done with understanding and are ready to go to work. So let me give you some tools.

CHAPTER 10

Choose Your Words
Change Your Life

I was in a project meeting with my superintendent, project manager, and subcontractors. We were reviewing progress on our twelve-week schedule and had ascertained that we were behind a week with four weeks to go. Being the optimist and knowing that going back to lay blame would not further my goals I began to strategize to do five weeks of work in four weeks. As I began to question my team on delivery of materials, answers on design issues and site logistics, the answer was clear. The attitude and language of the team was very negative and no one was engaged.

A survey of the answers started with "I tried," "The problem is," "If this would not have happened." Hopefully you can see what I see. The rest of the sentences were excuses. Men and companies were being paid to produce. Instead they all acted intelligent as they spoke the words of a teenager. In past chapters I used the term "psychological surrender." Using words like *tried*, *problem*, *but*, *if*, we are choosing to separate ourselves from the results. That is why I call it psychological surrender. These are victim words. You frame yourself has helpless and hopeless.

In this paragraph I hope to illustrate not only how the words we use beat us down psychologically but also how words can be used in a more proactive manner to help us live the life we choose. Focusing on words we use enable us to be better listeners, constantly sharpening our skills to choose. Choose the right words, choose the right times, choose whom we enjoy talking to and who we feel is more like-minded. So while I can write an entire book on language and words, let's focus on the three I alluded to above to prove my point

Try.

When you are getting paid to do a task, is this word really relevant? Trying is failure with honor. We use this word to feel our effort was noble. In fact we don't have to give any effort at all. By saying "I tried" we are covered with a comfortable blanket that makes us feel accomplished while we have actually accomplished nothing at all. Let's examine this word from the opposite perspective. Let's pretend that you worked all week and when it came time to be paid, there is no paycheck. Not to worry, your boss is there to tell you he tried his best to fund. Are you in any way comforted by the notion of him "trying"? Of course you're not. Yet I am willing to bet that you used this word no less than twenty times in a week. When you use this word, know that you are lying to yourself and anyone else who are depending on you.

You are forced to try when having to take a college course with less than adequate skills. Your life and occupation is not college. Your choices to this point have manifested in the life you are currently living. Your words must define a new life. I would suggest if you are comfortable using this word, you are not living the life you want. From this point on we are no longer trying. The reason is thirty minutes later we are saying "I tried" (past tense). This is when our brain tells the heart to give up and move on. Let's examine a scenario in how different words can bring different results.

The vice president of marketing wants to gather data for a sales meeting in four days. He announces on Monday morning that by Friday morning he needs sales for the past six months as well as demographics for sales. For added pressure he demands that the team establish a financial demographic for the stores and sales by three-mile radius, five-mile radius, and ten-mile radius. The executive has given you and two other coworkers the task to have this ready by Friday morning.

Typical Response and Outcome: The three employees bemoan the fact that this has been thrown on them. The three employees critique the management style of the executive. They establish responsibilities for necessary task. While some are qualified to do the work, personal commitments will keep them from dedicating the necessary time. Thus, when the executive meets with his team Wednesday afternoon they inform him, "We are having problems with gathering sales numbers for all stores as some stores report differently. We do not have enough time to verify all the data." They are going to *try* and do their best. When the meeting is over, the team is satisfied that they gave enough rationale (excuses) as to why they may fail. For good measure, they also gave the surrender word of "We are going to try." In their hearts and minds they are not committed to the outcome, so they stroke their ego by saying they tried.

What would happen if we used different words to manifest our choice? Let's look at how our outcome is changed by the words.

Using words to win: The three employees resented that they have been compromised but recognized that if it was easy, anyone can do it. The three reviewed the necessary task and agreed on responsibilities. Then they scheduled a Tuesday afternoon meeting to review issues and agree on a direction that can be implemented. Thus, when the executive meets with his team on Wednesday to check on progress, they inform him that while the data is not coming in as anticipated, they are in the process of using the year-to-date percentages to illustrate and they will note on the illustration where this method was used. Everyone on the team understands their role and they will have it correlated and put together one hour before meeting.

By using positive non-ambiguous language the team was constantly reinforcing their choice and commitment to deliver on a deadline. Once the choice was made to deliver, they did not let circumstances get in their way, nor did they speak using words to erode their resolve. They did not *try*, which leaves an undetermined outcome. They said they were *in the process and will get it done*. The vice president was grateful for their commitment and gave them half a day that Friday confident that his team would step up if ever called upon.

Words are very powerful. Especially the words we allow our conscious to speak to us. Once you are aware of the words and thoughts in your own head, you will be more aware of the words when people speak to you. You will be making a choice to choose words that will enhance your desired result or goal.

Problem.

Another word that I believe slowly erodes our resolve and renders us helpless is the word *problem.* What do you or someone really mean when they announce that they have a "problem"? When they are speaking of a personal internal issue, they use this word as another means of asking for help. However, in life when most people bring a problem to you, what they are really saying that it is your problem to deal with and they give up on finding solutions. Childishly it is almost like a game of hot potato. You have a problem that you feel is above your pay grade and the result is of no concern to you. So you conveniently announce that there is problem and you leave others to figure it out.

Hopefully you see the psychological surrender of this word. Next time you are in this situation, use the word *issue.* Everyone wants to be involved in the issue. When we have an issue, it automatically incites dialogue. People want to be part of solving issues because it is not someone's "problem." As a matter of wanting to empower people, I will try to guide my team on using words whether to speaking to clients or one another. Appreciate that when working with others on a collective goal, it is not advantageous to use the word *I* when you are a *we.*

But…

If…

"We almost got it done! But life happens. Imagine when explaining results we use the word *so?*

Example:

(Negative) We almost finished the siding, but it rained.

(Positive) At 4:00 p.m. it started to rain, so we tented off the last section so we could finish the siding. The premise is clear. Your choice of words as well as your comfort with words shapes your outcome. When you choose to refuse to use the words *but* or *if,* your measure of accountability to yourself will improve immeasurably and your choices will be clearer. When you choose a path, when you make goals to arrive at a designated place, you should choose to avoid using words like *but* or *if* as these words are sending your mind mixed messages that "if we don't achieve our goals, it is okay." As long as we attached some weak rationale after *but* or *if,* we will sound like eager executives.

In the event that this book or chapter is helping you understand that your words help reinforce and tear down your choices, know that science has proven when your words and thoughts are signals to your subconscious mind. Your conscious mind has a far smaller capacity as it is compared to the subconscious mind. For instance, people that begin to meditate and hold one conscious thought for five minutes will find their mind to be bouncing around in all strange directions. Subsequently your subconscious mind works in the opposite. That part of your brain will never fail you. This is the part of the brain that works in the way it was taught. Once taught, the subconscious mind will walk on autopilot. The subconscious ensures you breathe, walk, balance, dance, and yes, drive! Anyone who has driven for ten years and has worked at the same place knows where he is going. You can have a million thoughts going through your conscious mind while the radio is playing and you are looking at your phone. How did you get home? How did you operate your car? You have no memory of being aware of where you are going or how you got there? This is the power of the subconscious mind.

Thus, when you choose positive words continually, your mind listens and reacts. By constantly reinforcing your choices by choosing your words to reinforce and protect your choice, you are training your subconscious mind to help you. There are many books, scientific and esoteric, that can assist in validating what I am telling you. In the meantime, I ask that you trust the power of words and thoughts when making a choice and analyzing the results. What words did you use? Did the word hurt or reinforce your intended goal? Ironically when writing this book I had to constantly do my best (notice I did not say try) to use the correct words to make you aware of the point I am making.

In the future we will realize how much our own thoughts and words have shaped the proposition and outcome of our choices. Probably the best choice you can make is to contemplate and start listening to yourself and others speak every day. Once you are more aware, then maybe reading a book on the subconscious mind will help reinforce the awareness being presented in this chapter. Action speaks louder than words. Just know that your actions and reactions are governed by what you constantly tell your mind. Know that once accepted you have the ability to consciously and subconsciously affect the way you think and the results your thoughts manifest. Moreover, you can choose to use this power, or you can choose to ignore it. By the measure you are now up to chapter 10, I am confident you are ready to notice it! You take it from there.

CHAPTER 11

Who Is Making the Choice?
Ego vs. Spirit

Ego vs. spirit sounds deep? Sounds spooky? Certainly does not sound like anything going on inside of you. Well, it is. Some think of it as the angel and the devil on your shoulder. Some will think of it as Jimmy Cricket explaining the right thing to do. However you choose to simulate the voices inside your head, or the emotions going through you, you must acknowledge that both exist in all of us and have a major role in our decisions. Ironically, probably the most important decision we can make is which voice we will allow to speak to us. Although this dynamic can be viewed and communicated in several ways, we will use the words *spirit* and *ego* to delve deeper into the subject of voices and emotions running through us.

Spirit as described in the dictionary has many meanings and ways it can be used. The same condition exists when attempting to clearly define *ego*. We must use this as proof that we are attempting to simplify a very complex issue. In an effort to better understand the meaning of these two words as they will be used in this chapter, we can use other words to describe *spirit* (simple, kindness, larger view, giving, unselfish, confidence, we, humility, our angel on the shoulder); *ego* (complex, self-absorbed, small view, taking, selfish, insecurity, I, vanity, our devil on the shoulder). For the purpose of this chapter, accept the above words as an assimilation of the words *spirit* and *ego*.

Depending on where you are in life, to age and experience is in relation to who has your ear in a sense. For instance, if you are a self-absorbed fourteen-year-old who has had an easy life with no tragedy, the chances are larger that you listen to your ego rather than spirit. Conversely if you are a fifty-year-old who has had success and failure, married and divorced, had a dream job and no job, lost family members to illness and tragedy, more than likely the spirit will have a louder voice in forming an objective opinion to make a choice. Again we have no scorecard here. We only give the above situation to establish a common ground on the basis that a teenager and an older person are shaped by experience and have a difference in priorities. Basically when you are a teenager, everything matters—your hair, the weather, your clothes, commercials on the radio, people's tone of voice, facial expressions etc. You get the point. As a teenager you are now socially aware; thus, you are under the illusion that people are scrutinizing everything about you, as you are them. That is why it is so hard to reach a teenager. The spirit and ego do not communicate very well. That is not to say as you get older you acknowledge spirit. No. There is no guarantee that you will come to value spirit over ego. One more visual to assimilate the difference in this dichotomy. Imagine a rapper in a video with his Gucci clothes, driving his Bentley convertible throwing money out the window. This is your ego. Now imagine you are one of one hundred Buddhist monks living on a mountain with no money. Everyone dresses the same and takes care of one another. What they think, say, and do are the same; thus, they live in harmony. This is spirit.

Ego can be a very beneficial component to our mental makeup. For instance, anyone involved in competition will use ego as the basis to train and compete harder to prove "I am the best." Many positives can be derived by choosing to listen to this voice. This is the voice that speaks to your vanity. There is a part of you that believes if you attain a certain level, superiority will be established. Your spirit knows being the best is temporary; wanting to be the best is eternal.

Your ego projects your inner thoughts on to others. For instance, you care how you look; you analyze how others look. So you believe that people are doing the same to you. Probably the best example of the ego I describe is the tradition of going to church on Easter Sunday. For those of you who are not Christian, if you go to church once a year, this is the day you go. So knowing everyone will be there, the ego chooses to wear their best clothes to present the best of themselves as if this is who they really are. The ego is a deceiver. The ego will do anything for you not to recognize that you can live without it. To be clear, I am not against looking your best. The only difference between us, only you know if you are doing it for you or you're doing it for others. Another way to look at this dichotomy of the ego is who you want people to believe you are. Spirit is who you really are for better or worse and accepting that. Believe me when I tell you, there are very few people I have met in my short lifetime that is at peace with that last sentence.

The issue of ego vs. spirit becomes even further complex when they are viewed as the same. Earlier we used the example of the good that can come from ego, as in setting goals for competition. Who is talking when we want to give up? In the event you answered correctly, you are that much closer to understand this difficult concept that exist in all of us. The answer is of course the same person that set the goal, ego. Ego always defines everything via quantity. Ego is attracted to that which it can define. That is why we have titles at work. As we have discussed many times in this book, the sword cuts both ways. So ego limits your ability to accomplish the goal it created for you. Ego says you have worked hard enough; ego says forget it it's not worth it. Ego says you're not getting enough respect, not making enough money, not getting the credit you deserve. Be mindful. All these perceived slights have a quantity to them, or worse, a finial number! "I have had enough! You're not paying enough! I deserve more respect!" All these actions driven by emotion are ego based.

As much as we have all said these things at one time or another, and to be sure they are ego, do not forget the ego is a deceiver and a liar. So an interesting way to notice who is really talking is when you justify any action. "Well, I (key word) deserve the promotion.

I was here three years longer." The reason I made a scene is he disrespected me by (anything) you like. Whenever you have to justify your actions, 99 percent of the time the decision to act, as well as the decision to react, is ego based. Many of you are probably thinking of an incident over the last three days that you acted solely on ego without holding yourself accountable for lack of control. While reliving those moments is frustrating, we must hold ourselves accountable. We must admit that the deceiver is speaking to us to justify feeling uncomfortable or unhappy. So we will now address an ego situation and answer with spirit using what we have been made aware of in this book so far.

Robert worked as a carpenter for his company for seven years. Robert started as a laborer at twenty-three. Through hard work, he learned the trade and was making top carpenter pay in four years. Colleagues, upper management, and clients genuinely liked Robert. In his fifth year he was given an opportunity to run a carpentry crew due to his willingness to lead. By year 7 he was thirty, recently married, and just bought a house. Robert was confident in his own abilities and the possibility for advancement in the company. The opportunity arose where upper management was hiring a superintendent. The responsibility to coordinate not just carpenters but all trades would pay another $12,000 per year. Robert was confident his loyalty to the company would be rewarded as he excelled in technical knowledge and leadership. Besides, the company was hiring from the inside. One candidate was a laborer foreman who did not know as much. The other was a guy working under Robert as a lead carpenter.

Robert was not the successful candidate. Worse, the successful candidate was a man working under him. So now let's look at the insecure, selfish, small view of the situation as Rob is confronted with this perceived slight.

Dealing with the situation after using ego to guide you: Ego dictates that "they will pay for not respecting my abilities." Rob immediately lets those around him know that he will be soon looking for another job. "I have committed my future to this company and they never gave me a fair chance." Upon witnessing his attitude, other concerned opportunistic colleagues complained to upper management of his true feelings for the company and his intentions. When management sat down with Rob, his ability to show leadership went out the window and he became a victim of his employers. Knowing that no matter what he said, they were going to give the job to his coworker Robert went into the meeting with an opportunity to have his say and validate his feelings. Ego! In short order he came across as a bitter victim. When they told him he should look for another job but they would keep him working in the meantime, Robert responded with more indignation and ego. This not only caused him to be fired on the spot but also to forever be removed from the possibility of being rehired.

Dealing with the situation after using spirit to guide you: Spirit does not see a personal slight. Spirit sees this as an opportunity on so many levels. An opportunity to explore another company. An opportunity to further communication with ownership. An opportunity to show my men that I am leading that it is all about "what are you going to do about it" and work harder.

You see spirit is the opposite of ego. Where ego has a quantity for everything, spirit knows no quantity. Spirit wants to do whatever it takes to complete the goal. Spirit knows no limits. Spirit never quits. That is why everything is an opportunity. Robert never complained. He immediately requested a meeting with upper management and owners on his terms. While management was not happy with breaking protocol, they did respect Robert as a team member and went to the meeting with an open mind. When Robert was given the opportunity to speak, he spoke with gratitude for the opportunity to hone his skills with company. He expressed gratitude for the opportunity to start a family and buy a house because of the company's success that benefited him. Triumphantly he stated that he had every intention of procuring the next superintendent spot that opened up. Robert was very clear to ownership that his responsibilities at home and on the job have increased. Thus, he asked that they find more opportunities for him to earn more money—whatever was available, overtime, weekend work, working in the owner's home. Lastly, he asked each member at the meeting for a tip on what he can work on to ensure he is successful the next go-round. While management was relieved and inspired by their rejected employee, they did offer advice to take some elective college courses to improve his computer skills. Some had asked that he focus on his writing. Robert accepted all critique with appreciation. After a quick break, ownership created ways for Robert to work with a tutor for writing and computer skills three days a week for two hours.

In past chapters we looked at cause and effect, accountability, I have no choice, goals and consequences. So using the first six chapters let's illuminate what we have come to be aware of. For the purpose of reflecting we will discuss the egotistical choice.

First, the circumstance was not getting the promotion. Second came the choice to react negatively to company and coworkers or as we describe it cause. Third came the effect, Robert was told he should find other employment but he would work and be paid until such time. Fourth, when Robert had the opportunity reflect and acknowledge his part in all his bad choices to this point, Robert did not acknowledge accountability. Thus, he lashed out on the owners because he felt he had no choice as the other candidate had already gotten the job. Robert felt he had no choice. The amazing thing is that none of these things would have happened if he had a clearly defined goal. Robert wanted the job. Ego told him he was entitled so he never let *desire* take shape. Conversely, in the example of spirit, all the facets of choice were addressed. So with one good choice followed another, then another. So am I saying that spirit is the best way to make all of your decisions?

Before we answer that question let's look at the negative side of spirit. In the author's opinion, having spirit is not a good thing; rather, it is a great thing. One of the highest compliments you can pay someone is to say "They have spirit." As we have already discussed spirit does not quantify a limit. Spirit believes all things are possible if you're committed to not giving up. So when you are living a life where your choices affect many others' life, spirit is not the only remedy. In these rare issues ego is needed. In the case of my company rise and fall, the decision to start was made of ego. Ego set the first goal and we were off. Thirteen years later when I really needed to make ego-based decision I could not. My programming was already "No limits," "Never give up," Never Quit." So when a little self-preservation would have been prudent, the ego was not convincing enough to sway. While my ego was always there, my spirit has usually guided me and up until this point always won, even then ego said enough is enough, quit. So what is the right voice to listen to? Because this book is on choice, I will say you choose. Note with benefit that there are roughly 1.4 million people incarcerated on any given day. After reading this chapter, I hope you agree with the author's opinion that 99 percent of the 1.4 million are there from a series of ego-based choices.

So now we are back to honesty and accountability. These virtues are neither spirit nor ego, just used when needed. Think of your mind as a courtroom. Spirit and ego are opposing attorneys arguing their case in front of Honesty the Judge. Of course to make sure the rules of the court are being followed we have the bailiff, integrity (accountability). Admit it is kind of fun to observe your own mind when you are aware of this condition. Spirit argues in the subjective while the tricky ego uses objective arguments to gain favor with reason. For this reason I believe the most important person in the courtroom is Honesty the Judge. Both spirit and ego can be helpful and harmful. You just need the judge to tell you who has the floor. Anytime a decision is made, a new trial begins and the arguments start. Let's do a quick trial that starts for every smoker every day.

Judge: We are here today to decide whether or not we smoke.

Ego: (Using rationale) Why must we waste time on the matter? Smoking is our weakness. No matter how hard we try, circumstances of the day will make us give in. Why do we know this? Because it happens every day. Thinking you can endure pain to get through this is, well, egotistical. Now stop this debate at once and light up!

Spirit: Do not believe my clever friend, Ego. He will have you believe if you do something wrong long enough, it becomes right. You are more powerful than you realize! Your power is endless if you just stop listening to the objective limits of Ego over there. Quit today and never give up on your ability to make the right decision in spite of your needs and wants.

EGO: (Applause) Very inspiring! Look at that cigarette and say you don't want to light up!

Spirit: Objection, your honor. I do not have a clean lung to show. Can we stick to oratory to keep a level playing field?

Judge: Bailiff, please direct the mind to leave the room with cigarettes in it until we hear all oral arguments. The entire direction of staring at the cigarettes shall be stricken from the record.

Ego: Forget it. This is a bullshit argument. We have been here one thousand times before. Sure I want to quit. Someone has to be real. You will be smoking by two p.m. and you know it.

Spirit: If you only believe in you the way I do, you would know it is not easy but worth it.

Now you do not have to be a smoker to empathize with that argument. The discussion could be regarding a diet, relationship, or career issues. This chatter and conversation go on sometimes without you being aware. The paradox of the mind is that the mind must use itself to understand itself. As difficult as this is to grasp, we are reading a book to understand ourselves better. So I have to believe if we approach this and all new endeavors with spirit, we will find more answers. To approach reason through spirit we must be unassuming and untainted. So one more analogy on the understanding and meaning of spirit.

To truly understand spirit, think of it as the mind of a baby. There is no perception of time. There is calculation of limits to how much you cry or you love. Every new thing you see is a wonder. Every new experience is a measure of gratitude for being in this place at this time. To a child all things are possible. Anything the mind can imagine can be created. When you are a child, this is a reality. You remember just loving an ice cream cone. You visualized it, you thought about it, you loved it…and it came to you. Moreover, you were grateful.

Then little by little, day by day our ego tricked us to expect the ice cream. Then expecting was not enough. We had to have the biggest. Then the biggest was not enough. We had to have it more often. Attempt to explain this premise to a four-year-old and he would just tell you he loves ice cream and he is happy that you do too.

No matter how old you are, or where you are in your life, to really attempt to view life differently, or analyze your choices from a different point of view, make an effort to view or approach a situation with the fresh view of a child. Feed your spirit with new knowledge and stimulating new experiences. Once you push yourself to new situation, be sure to view it from the eyes of a child. You may not change but you will be a happier version of you. Regardless of your age, it would seem we have much to learn from a four-year-old.

As I mentioned in the beginning paragraph this is a very complex subject to tackle in such a small chapter. The author's hope is that I have been able to illustrate the differences in a manner that you can perfect in your own mind. The objective was never to get you to think a certain way. The objective was to get you to think. Think about who is doing the talking in your mind. Who is winning? Where does honesty and integrity belong in the decision making process. We have to believe that this chapter has opened our eyes to an insight that can make a difference. Imagine that once you see how imperfect a process it is to make any decision, we just may lighten up on judging others.

CHAPTER 12

Observing Choice and Applying Judgment

There is a social media post that states, "Before you judge my decision, you should at least be aware of my options." While this statement is entirely on point, applying this to everyday life takes away the dishonest guilty pleasure of you are somehow better. You're not. Worse the act of applying judgment and opinions on others takes you away from the issues that matter most. You! Thus, in this chapter we will view how the misuse of our thoughts and energies can hold back our own ability to make good decisions.

Before we jump into judgment, I would like to explain what is meant by judgment when analyzing someone else's choice. First off, opinion is not judgment. No need to break out the dictionary for this one. Bottom line is if I say I do not like your shirt, this is my opinion. Had I said I do not like your shirt and that is why you cannot come into my home, that is judgment. Due to the new way of thinking and acting, the propagandists have made us believe they are one and the same. Your opinions on matters may change due to circumstances and education. You can always change your opinion unless you are a conservative politician in which case the media will remind you daily that you cannot. I digress. We all change our opinions on issues, products, people, and a whole host of other parts of life. The important thing is to recognize that your opinions and feelings can and will change. Your opinion is no different from anyone else. Subject to conditioning, exposure, education, and experiences. Thus, they really should not matter.

My wife and I embarked to have a child out of wedlock at the ages of fifteen and eighteen. As you would imagine, we received opinions from people of all ages. I am certain a great many people had opinions that I did not know, nor did we hear. Suffice to say of all the opinions I heard none were living my circumstance with my history in my time. So while half of the opinions were well intentioned, in a very practical sense they are meaningless. May sound obtuse or cruel, sometimes the truth is. We all have opinions. What make them vicious are people reacting negatively to them, and judgment.

Judgment is the act of taking your opinion and acting on it. Hence, had someone said if you have this child I will no longer be in your life and go through with it, that is judgment. The act of purposely ignoring someone based on your opinion, or worse the opinion of others, is judgment. When you do something or say something to hurt someone based on your opinions of them, that is judgment. As you can see there is a huge difference between opinions and judgment. Opinions are your own and they are benign even if they are outrageous. Your opinion can change. Once you apply judgment, once you act, your actions affect others. This can never change. This cannot be taken back. As we will see the understanding between the two and choosing what to apply makes a huge difference in our lives moving forward.

To be clear, I have run men and owned a company for over twenty years. I can honestly say that judgment is a huge part of success and failure. So the choice is very real with very real consequences. All managers and owners in every business in every country must apply judgment. To be sure many people not in this position must think it feels wonderful and powerful to take the fate of a man or women's month (not their lives) and adversely and positively affect the outcome. Believe this, if you believe nothing else, it's not. I never took hiring or firing another person lightly. In fact when things were great and I would tell people that I wanted out in 2010 when I was forty, people always wanted to know why. My response was always the same. I hate being responsible for people's lives. Trust me when I say that there is a burden when you have people's financial fate in your hands and a $120,000 payroll every two weeks. You may imagine how that feels directly. The good does not outweigh the bad. The importance of this anecdote is to know how deeply I felt about the unavoidable predicament of judgment. Even though I look at the bright side of all issues. One man fired means a new guy hired. Judgment of any kind deteriorates a man's clarity and soul. We all do it. Men and women, we do what we have to do. So now that we have discussed the difference between opinion and judgment, as well as the exception to the rule being a business owner, let's get down to business on how judgment clouds our decision.

First and foremost issue with judgment is that it takes positive thoughts on your decisions and choices and focus on negative thoughts to someone else. So imagine your life as walking forward in a straight line. This is life, so you have to dodge some things that come your way. When you go opposite of where your thoughts and actions need to be, you are looking behind you and not seeing things clearly as to what is coming at you. This analogy mainly applies to ages sixteen to thirty, but for those with less experience at real life we tend to dwell on things that do not matter. Worse, to justify wasting our time, we throw a cherry on the wasted energy called judgment of others.

Since it is not in my nature to beat around the bush, let's get right to it. Judgment of others does not make you a better person. How can you focus on your issues while you are distracted with looking at others and what they do? Worry about you, not on who? We must embrace the logic that pointing out what we do not like in others and treating them accordingly is not a positive life choice. Conversely, being mindful of the wasted energy of judgment can ensure that you spend more time on the issues that advance your life. In other words, talking with your friend for twenty minutes as to why you are not inviting Susan to your party is a complete waste of valuable time and mind-set.

At this time I would like you to take a moment and review and acknowledge events over the past three years. How many of you have allowed opinions to become judgments. Now be honest, if you had to be in the same situation being one to three years smarter, would you act the same? For most the answer is of course no! Moreover, I am willing to bet that some of you wish you had that moment back. The good news is we have opened our mind to dealing the enemy within. You! Your issue was not in knowing the difference between opinion and judgment but knowing there was a choice to make that could have long-term effects on your life. Just stopping long enough to consider that a decision must be made will put you in a position to make a better decision. By choosing your thoughts, you are controlling your words and actions. Be careful moving forward of allowing your opinion to become judgments.

I recently watched a time travel movie where the males of the family had the ability to port through time. What an amazing power to have and share to affect all in a positive manner. Most profound was what he asked his son to do with this power. Live every day twice! He explained that every day goes by so fast and we don't acknowledge the beauty in the simple things in life. Worse this disconnect with life and source makes us irritable. Then anxiety sets in because we do not know what will happen next. The totality of it all keeps us on edge. When we are on edge, we make rash judgments!

Thus, he advised his son that as soon as the day was done, live the day again. Only this time with no edge as there will be no anxiety and there will be the opportunity to make better judgments to affect a more positive future. Amazingly simple. Beautiful message.

Although we do not have the power to change the course of yesterday and to a lower extent today. We do have the faculty to ensure a better tomorrow by choosing to acknowledge today. Of course we cannot travel time. What is being suggested is spending fifteen minutes at the end of the night or early morning before getting out of bed and reliving the day in your mind without the feeling of stress and reliving the good parts and think about the changes you would like to make. The point is we have the power to make better judgments when we work at first expecting to make better judgments and second to acknowledge if we can choose to work on losing anxiety.

All this is borne out of choice. Probably the most dynamic choice. This is the choice you're not aware of!

Now let's take a very personal, common sense approach to judgment. Everyone reading this book has received judgment by someone—teacher, students, coworkers, and family members. Moreover, my psychic abilities tell me that you received this judgment without proper understanding (see first paragraph of the chapter). Can you for a moment remember how alone you felt in the injustice of it all? Can you remember how suffocating the air of misunderstanding and resentment and anger was? Willing to bet you relived some of those ugly emotions. Made you feel pretty bad all over again. Everyone reading this book can empathize with this paragraph. Yet all of us have repeated this atrocity on another. Let that sink in for a moment.

A quick anecdote, my wife experienced something that ties into the judgment and subsequent emotions we discussed in the past paragraph. My wife was a mother at fifteen. She was a mother of two at eighteen. So this is how senseless judgment works. Being a mother of two at eighteen years old, Danielle was judged by her peers as not being worthy of camaraderie. To put it bluntly, her perceived friends abandoned her. Well, at least when we moved to the Jersey suburbs when she was twenty and our daughter was starting kindergarten. So clearly other moms would gravitate to a mother of two. Absolutely none. All offers to assist in any way were rebuked. No one knew she had a husband. I work any available hour. No one knew she was a responsible, conscientious mom. No one knew that she was living the same life as they were. The reason no one knew? Judgment. They assumed she was irresponsible because she had children so young. They assumed she had no husband because they had never seen one. Basically everything they thought was wrong. That did not matter. They might have had a negative opinion based on what they perceived. The tragedy we all experienced was they acted on their opinion. That action became judgment.

In being honest we can all think of a time when we allowed our opinions to become action, hence judgment. I believe that the author has sufficiently explained the difference between opinion and judgment. You are probably asking, what do opinions and judgment have to do with choice? Everything! Our behavior and subsequent choices are directly symbiotic to our thoughts and actions toward others. Human beings as a society will always dictate what they tolerate. This relationship is never discussed, yet it makes up a larger view of how we see the world we live in. Simple analogy. In some societies having multiple wives is tolerated and allowed such as Muslims and Mormons. Naturally in the Muslim and Mormon communities they dictate laws and societal norms to validate what they tolerate. Hence, subconsciously we all dictate what we tolerate. Recognize in some way we do this to validate issues that require explanation. Hence judgment. You grow up with nefarious behavior going on around you. You see it, and partake of doing it to others because you're happy it's not you. Then you spend an unusual amount of time telling everyone else why you did something you would never want to happen to you. You *dictate* (do) what you *tolerate* (what has happened and what you never want to happen to you).

When we acknowledge this premise, then we must take stock of our goals, desires, and wishes for our future. Our thoughts and ability to think outside the social norms will not get you a lot of friends. What you will acquire is the ability to see things in a non-egotistical light. Your ability to make better choices will be acutely better as you will be practicing almost every minute of every day. Seeing all sides of an issue will make you wiser. Again just the act of thinking before acting makes our ability to make better choices. Please note when I say better choices, I do not mean the right one. A better choice in line with your goals in life as well as your stated objectives to meet those goals. On a personal note I will say that when I contemplate my decisions, I am usually happy with those decisions. Conversely when I make rash judgments, I am never happy as that is not the way I want to be.

So that is why acknowledging this chapter is paramount in moving forward. We have lived with opinions that change, so stay open. We have all lived with the effects of someone acting on an uninformed opinion about us (judgment). Treat others how we want to be treated. We acknowledge how societal norms shape our behavior, yet we know that social norms deliver norms. We are reading this book to make better choices to assist in extraordinary results. When we control our thoughts, we control our actions. Forty percent of our thoughts are opinions on people, issues, and situations. Your mental activity will not change. How you train your mind to form opinions will greatly affect your ability to make good, consistent choices. These more cerebral choices will undoubtedly affect innocent people for the better. Your opinions will shape your actions. Your judgments positively or adversely affect you and others. Thus, when all these factors affect your choice, the more you have the factors in line, the more beneficial your choices will be.

CHAPTER 13

Are We Ready?

While we may be kicking ourselves for some of our past choices, know that I am always grateful for today. Today allows yet another opportunity to learn from yesterday. Know that your life is one goal, one choice, one decision away from being completely different if you choose. You have to admit that it is very exciting to have new tools in which to make a new creation if you desire.

Upon reading this book we are not guaranteed to make better choices. At the very least we will know we are making a choice that will lead to further consequences. In the event that the intended benefits are recognized, then we will acknowledge our role when we are making good choices and or putting ourselves in a position to fail.

The insights that have been discovered can only serve to benefit us in the future if we are willing to be honest with ourselves. In fact, without honesty there will be nothing in this book to apply to your life. People often hunger for truth but seldom like the way it tastes. Your future depends on your ability to be honest with yourself.

Many reading this book will be or are young parents. Some may already have grown children. Know that they will be or are analyzing your choices. So whether you make good ones or bad ones, be honest with yourself so you can be honest with others. The honesty factor will ensure you are on the right track. Who knows, your honesty will come across as sincerity when you are trying to help someone else. To be sure, you will never contemplate or review a choice the same way again. Having said that, the reader would not receive the intended benefits without being honest.

So for this last chapter I will use a scenario that affects us all. This situation changes in effect as we grow older.

We are going to study the Murphys who had not taken a vacation in three years. Ironically the reason it took them three years was the crippling financial effect of their last vacation. As we tell their story, we may bounce back from this year to three years ago. We will do this to aid ourselves in future decisions. The past when viewed through honest eyes can give a tremendous insight to help with future decisions. Through analyzing the Murphys' plight, we will tie in and mention as many chapters of this book as we can. For the record, we are undergoing this exercise to review and incorporate what we have read. The outcome of the Murphys is right for the Murphys. Again the choice matters in relation to your life and your goals. The author is not delivering a counterintuitive view on choice by telling you what the right one was.

Jane Murphy asked her husband Jim to consider joining her whole family on a Disney vacation to celebrate their parents' fortieth wedding anniversary. Jane explained that the other brothers, sisters, grandchildren, as well as some cousins and an uncle, were traveling to enjoy this very special occasion with her parents. Jane did due diligence and figured the four days away for their family of five would cost $5,000. There would be no discounts as the kids were fifteen, twelve, and ten. Jim immediately responded that it is March and the anniversary is not till end of August. Jane stated that she assessed the cost at today's prices. The closer we get to the date, the more it would cost. Jim gave a defeated look and walked away. Jane understood and did not push.

The reason that Jane did not push was she realized how far they have come since the financial debacle of three years ago. At that time they had been living month to month. Jim worked as a super for a national publicly traded homebuilder, but their youngest daughter Rose would be going to kindergarten that September. This would enable Jane to get a job in publishing again. They discussed the pros and cons of taking on such an expense on the credit card. Conversely they were faced with the fact that the kids were not getting any younger. So they decided that a memory was worth the risk of sacrificing their goals for six months to pay off the credit card bills. Besides, who knows, Jane may get a job quickly and that income could immediately erase the new debt. Despite having fixed financial goals they figured they would expedite their vacation a year early.

Jim booked a six-day stay at a resort in the Bahamas for some quality family time. The trip was paid courtesy of the credit card, $6,000. When Jim returned to work a week later, he was greeted with a two-week severance check and a letter of recommendation. The housing market soured to a point that demanded layoffs. Jane was unsuccessful in landing a job. Unemployment aided with Jim working side jobs and worked until November. Prior to their August excursion the Murphys were living month to month. Although they did own their home and had some equity, mortgaging a home, two cars, as well as pay for life insurance and a small college fund, did not allow for extras. Any family with young kids understands this dilemma. The Murphys as well knew they were taking a risk when they decided to throw caution to the wind.

Most reading this book knows what comes next. The Murphys juggled to find ways to stay on top of bills despite less money coming in. Worse the monthly reminder of the two-hundred-dollar minimum payments on the credit card. By the end of November heading into December reality had set in. With winter coming side jobs would be all but gone. The housing industry never hires from November to March. So Jim's opportunity for employment without relocating or extensive travel was narrow to be kind. Ultimately Jim and Jane fell into despair as they had maxed credit cards and were unable to give the children the Christmas they had grown accustomed to. They felt if they just stayed the course and kept juggling, things would get better. Besides, what choice did they have? Life had thrown a curveball and they would make the best of it. The Murphys decided to leave it in God's hands and they would get through it together. Despair in December turned into dismay in March. Their credit had gone from 780 to 660 due to late payments on mortgage, credit cards, and cars. Worse was the fact that credit card companies hit the Murphys with exorbitant late fees and raised their interest rate. Of course the Murphys tried conventional lending, but no help was offered. They were slowly drowning and they knew it. By end of April between credit cards, cars, utility, and mortgage debt they owed $11,000 in debt including the $4,800 for their $6,000 vacation seven months earlier. Jim or Jane was hesitant to ask for any help until either one received gainful employment.

Two months later Jim was hired back by his old company at his same salary despite the ten-month layoff. Jane was successful getting part-time work for a national retailer who just opened in her town. So Jim and Jane had gotten to a point one year later from there ill-fated vacation to set positive goals to get themselves back on track. Jim's dad lent them money interest free for two years to catch up on all old payments to help restore their credit. The plan was in place that once credit score was creeping up in six months the Murphys would trade in their cars for older cars and use the excess money to pay down all other bills. Jane and Jim figured with sticking to the plan put in place to achieve the goals, they could be debt free with the exception of their mortgage in two years. Jim realized that he could not win today. Conversely, if he did not choose his consequences, he would be victim of the circumstance of making one wrong decision at the wrong time.

So ironically with five months to go to finish their "get back" goal, life pulls them away. While Jim and Jane were still not comfortable, they could see the light at the end of the tunnel. Jim had been here before. Through living and reflecting on the cause and effect of what had happened to their lives due to their financial hardship was his fault. Could he have predicted a layoff? Yes. Did he know that it was against his goals and irresponsible to make the trip at that time? Yes! He used cause and effect. Behind every effect, his decision was the cause.

Only now things were different. The Murphys had faced adversity that we all do at one time or another. This time they were not nervous. They knew the worst of it and knew how to choose to avoid the unpleasantness. So upon discussing the pros and the cons of the venture with common sense and rationale the Murphys made a decision, or shall I say the Murphys were disciplined enough to let the goals make the decisions. They decide that Jane would attend with their twelve-year-old daughter and split a room with her sister and young six-year-old daughter. Plus, Jane would use her college friend's year-round hopper passes who lived in Orlando. The entire trip would cost the Murphy's less than $2,000. While Jim and Jane did not pick the circumstance, their choices picked the consequences. Jim was proud that he was able to keep his ego in check and tune out the bogus thoughts of how other family members would think of him for making such a different decision. You are the choice you make, so the Murphys made choices they could live with.

In the above anecdote of the Murphys' vacation plight, we can all see ourselves in this scenario. Even if you were a college student that needed a grade and went on a three-day excursion with friends, you pay the price and you must *learn* from it. So are you ready? I will make this prediction. While you were reading the story, you heard my words and saw your life? My prediction is you are absolutely ready to challenge yourself to be aware of your decisions and their consequences. Knowing that you are the choices you make is a very tough way to live. That would mean that you would actually spend the rest of your life with the pressure that you are conducting an orchestra that makes up the sounds of your life. Sure, someone may sneeze during your greatest performance, but you still choose how you move forward.

Choosing the last paragraph for this book was probably the easiest of all. These pages have given us a blueprint on how to objectively and subjectively analyze our decisions and behavior. The purpose of the book was never to make a map, rather to merely point in the direction and reinforce that it's possible for you to control how you travel and what your final destination will be. You are the choices you make. You may be happy with the life your choices have manifested for you, or you may be miserable. Either way, the results come from your choices. In the highly unlikely event that you read this book and believe your life would be different if other people made different choices, then please read it again. You obviously missed a few critical sentences. Seriously, while you may not have a map, this book destroyed the mystery. You are the choices you make. Period. For our final analogy, think of your life as a book. You may not pick the cover, the paper, the font, or the ink but you do get to choose the words, for better or worse. Fortunately for us, we have a guideline, or a manifesto on how to make and analyze choices to reinforce our dreams. I hope this book aids us all in writing the best possible chapters of our life.

ABOUT THE AUTHOR

Brian Abbey grew up in the Bronx, New York and moved to New Jersey in 1993. He has been married to his wife, Danielle, for over 27 years. They are raising their children Ashley (26), and Brian (23), together in their home in south Jersey. He and his wife stayed and operated a 20-million dollar construction company, building national chain restaurants for over 15 years. They continue to reside in New Jersey with their five dogs. They also have a residence in Arizona. They are die-hard football fans and enjoy big Italian family holidays.

CPSIA information can be obtained at www.ICGtesting.com
Printed in the USA
BVOW05s1434061215

429476BV00003B/176/P